Awakening Your Feminine Spirit

Finding Balance, Purpose, and Strength

Stacie Ivey

Ivey Leaf Publishing
Albuquerque, New Mexico

An Ivey Leaf Publishing Publication
All rights reserved

Copyright 2017 by Stacie Ivey (stacieivey.com)

Published and distributed in the United States by:

 Ivey Leaf Publishing
Albuquerque, NM 87122

Editor: Amy Collette
Cover Design: Createspace by Amazon
Interior Design: Nancy Rynes and Ted Roach
Cover Photo: Oleh Slobodeniuk/Getty Images
Author Photo: Charles Lebeau

Published 2017
Printed in the United States of America

Ivey, Stacie
Awakening Your Feminine Spirit: Finding Balance, Purpose and Strength
ISBN-13: 978-0998180106
ISBN-10: 0998180106
LCCN: 2016917876
BISAC: Body, Mind & Spirit / Healing / General,
Self-Help / Spiritual

DEDICATION

To my beautiful, creative, intelligent and talented
children, Karenna and Aidan.
I am blessed and honored to be your mother and look
forward to watching your continued unfoldment as you enjoy
life and share your unique gifts with the world.

Stacie Ivey

TABLE OF CONTENTS

Stacie Ivey

DEAR READER,

We are living in a transcendent time unlike any other time on our planet. As women we are rising, like the Phoenix from the ashes. The shift is here and we feel it deep within. It is a calling to heal completely and release what is holding us back to step into our true purpose. This is the time for us to come together as women, own our greatness and reclaim our power. When we allow our internal light to shine, we become radiant and unstoppable.

This book is a guidepost through your journey of self-discovery. Whether you desire healing, deeper meaning and purpose, connected relationships, sacred love or are looking for ways to stay centered in the mist of chaos, this is a companion into the processes of letting go (sacred surrender), returning to your body (sacred embodiment), and opening your conscious awareness (sacred expansion) so you can live the life of your dreams. Simply open to believing everything is possible.

As you read through the pages of this book, you will explore practical thoughts and experiential opportunities offered as invitations to deepen your connection with the Divine Feminine, Sacred Mother and Goddess. She is beauty, compassion, forgiveness, receptivity and unconditional love. You will learn how to process your healing, embody your feminine essence, understand your energy, trust your intuition, and own your personal power. Everything you need or want is already embedded within. I feel blessed and honored you are here.

With so much love,

Stacie

Stacie Ivey

INTRODUCTION

"The energy that moves life is the force of the Feminine. She is unstoppable. She is the source of all life, the mover of blood, the breather of breath, the flow of the river's water. The Feminine is life. We can feel Her moving and living in any moment and we are open to Her, or as Her."
~David Deida

She comes as a calling, a sort of bubbling from within, tapping lightly at first and asking gently for you to listen. You ignore her for a while and she allows it. Eventually her call gets louder and stronger and she will not permit you to ignore her call any longer. Her love for you is so penetrating and unconditional that She waits until she knows you are ready and when you are, you know it. You know the call because it comes from the deepest, most vulnerable parts of your soul. When you are ready, you hear her say,

"Now is the time...
Now is the time for you to become who you are meant to be.
Now is the time for you to stop playing small so that others feel comfortable around you.
Now is the time to say no to the people and ideas that have been holding you back.
Now is the time to release your beliefs about who you are and to open up to your greatness.
Now is the time for you to shine and to step into the wholeness of you."

Now it is time on our planet for an awakening to occur, a realization that we are more than this body, more than this name we were given at birth, more than our family of origin and more than the culture and religion we were raised in. We

1

are so much more, in such a Divine, beautiful and fiery way that words cannot even describe. Our minds cannot comprehend this Divine grace, but our souls can. We are ready, now more than ever before, and She is coming.

*She is our Divine Mother and She is each of us collectively
and individually at the level of our souls.
She is coming in a way that transcends all belief.
She presents herself as an inner knowing, that somewhere,
each of us knew all along.
She is within and of our souls.
She wants to be heard.
She is beauty itself.
She is all-encompassing, yet subtle.
She is our Divine Mother.
She invites us to wisdom.
She invites us to surrender the old structures, systems and routines.
She invites us to freedom.
She invites us to be in gratitude for this great life.
She invites us to open to the grace that resides within all of us.
She is patiently waiting for us to remember the truth of
who She is and who we are.
She has been ready and She knows we are ready now.*

For many years there has been a spiritual longing for our return to inner peace and our deep internal connection to each other and the natural world. Our desire is to feel love so intimately, in all its capacity and forms. We want to experience the sacred embrace of the Divine, to live authentically, and to feel whole.

Growing up, we were taught about the masculine side of God, but what about the feminine side? What happened to her, our Divine Mother? Could the loss of her be the reason we feel so disconnected, alone and afraid? As an adopted child, I have been touched by this question through the separation and the return back to my own biological mother.

MY STORY

I was an infant born without my biological tribe into another tribe. There wasn't the welcoming ceremony I deeply longed for and needed at the moment of my birth, which was the embrace by and connection to my biological mother and father. In my transition from my mother's womb to the physical world, the hospital nurses immediately removed me from my mother, and my father was not known. They prevented my mother from holding me so that she wouldn't get attached and change her mind about the adoption. They believed that I, as an infant, had no awareness and would therefore have no memory of this catastrophic and profoundly impactful separation.

In an instant, everything that was familiar to me over the course of the nine months in my mother's womb was immediately removed. I lost her scent, the sound of her voice, and the resonant beating of her heart. The wound I experienced was deep and primal.

When I left the hospital two days after my birth to begin my life with my new adoptive parents, I was immediately welcomed and accepted as a new member of the family, as if I were exactly the same as a biological child. I was loved fully and completely.

However, there was an unmistakable wound that I carried with me. My newly adoptive mother told me I cried continuously for months. After my chronic and consistent crying continued for long enough, she took me to my doctor. At first he told her that's what babies do. Then it continued for a while longer and a more drawn-out period of time. Eventually, my doctor didn't know what to do with me, so he diagnosed me with colic and prescribed a medication to stop me from crying. The medication created the desired effect and numbed me enough to make me stop crying. From that experience, I also learned it was subconsciously necessary to numb parts of myself so that I wouldn't have to feel the pain, physically, mentally and emotionally.

I grew up always knowing I was adopted and always wondering who I was. I didn't have a baseline to draw from for the question, "Who am I?" because I didn't know anything about where I came from. I didn't know who I looked like, who I acted like, or anything about my family of origin. The only facts I knew were that my mother was 19, had red hair, and wanted me to be raised Catholic. I had no pictures or anything else to go by.

Additionally, there was an underlying fear that I carried regarding my adoptive mother. I believed she was afraid that I may not fully and completely love her and I was afraid of losing her if she didn't think I loved her, but I did love her. She also feared other people's judgments toward her for not being able to have her own children and because of that I grew up being told, "Don't tell anyone you're adopted." Unfortunately for my adoptive mother, there were multiple unavoidable inconsistencies to this secret I was being asked to keep as a child. I have red hair, green eyes, fair skin and am tall. I look very Irish/English. My mother, conversely, has dark hair, brown eyes, olive Italian skin, and is very petite. Even though we are both considered "Caucasian," we look very different. To compensate for that visible difference and because my adoptive parents were always asked, "Where did her red hair come from?" I was told by my mother, "If anyone asks where your red hair came from, just tell them it's from your father's side of the family."

At the age of five, we moved from where I was born in Pittsburgh, Pennsylvania across the country to Tucson, Arizona. At the age of 10, we returned to Pittsburgh for a week to visit my adoptive paternal grandmother just before she passed. Being back in Pittsburgh five years after we moved and old enough to know more of who I thought I was and what I wanted, I was plagued with wondering who my birth mother was, with tons of Catholic guilt to go along with it. I could never bring up what I was thinking about as we walked through the department stores, food stores and restaurants of Pittsburgh. If I did, I knew my adoptive mother would feel horrible and make me feel horrible for even thinking about my biological mother. Everywhere we went, I looked for women who would be approximately 29 with red hair. The Dr. Seuss book, "Are You My Mother?" became my personal story and I couldn't stop thinking about her. I never found her then.

Time passed and I went on with my life in Arizona. I had a good childhood with very loving, generous and kind parents. We went "glamping" in our Coachman motor home with my parents camping group monthly, took trips twice a year to a beach in Mexico, and lived on a golf course with a backyard pool. I was active in the church youth group, wrote for the school newspaper, played tennis and was in the color guard for the band. I was never supposed to discuss being adopted, yet I magically seemed to find all the other kids who were also adopted. We became friends and I revealed my secret under wraps to only those I trusted would not tell my mother that I told our secret to.

I confided in my Aunt Judy throughout my childhood that I would search for my birthmother one day. I thought about my biological mother on and off, especially on my birthdays. I could never tell my adoptive mother I had those thoughts because I worried it would emotionally destroy her. When I turned 18, I knew I could start looking but I didn't allow myself to look yet. I was busy starting college and beginning my life. It wasn't until after I got married that I became serious about my search. Along the way I met the occasional acquaintance who was also adopted. One such acquaintance was a friend of my husband's. She had found her birthmother through a woman who helped adoptive children find their birth mothers out of California. She gave me her phone number and I called. I was 27.

The woman I called was gentle, loving and a birth mother herself. She asked me, "Where were you adopted?" I told her Pennsylvania and she proceeded to tell me she only worked with California cases but had the name of a contact in Pennsylvania. She gave me another woman's name and phone number and wished me luck. I thanked her and hung up the phone, promptly calling the next phone number.

The next woman was also a birth mother, even more helpful than the first. She asked me, "Who did your adoption?" I told her and she then proceeded with a long explanation of the history of adoptions with the woman who did my adoption and then became an adoption agency. She told me I would need to contact the courts of Alleghany county and request that an intermediary be assigned to my case. She emphasized I must be very specific in my request and state that the intermediary must not be from the adoption agency I went through because they have a core belief that adoptive children should not be reunited with their birth mothers. She said, "If they are to be assigned to your case, they won't help you."

"What, really?" I asked. I was in shock that this was true still today. "Ok," I responded. "I will do as you say." I wrote my letter to the court to ask for an intermediary to be appointed that was not a part of the adoption agency that I was associated with. Within a few weeks, I was contacted by a woman named Deb. She told me she was assigned to my case and asked me to send proof that I was who I was. I said ok and then I hesitated. I did not want my adoptive mother to feel as if I were abandoning her. The Catholic guilt and shame was arising again. I temporarily stopped my search. I also worried about who my birthmother might be and prepared myself for the possible worst-case scenarios: "What if she was a drug addict, prostitute, homeless, or worse yet, what if she wants nothing to do with me and rejects me all over again?"

Two weeks later, the intermediary, Deb called me again. She said, "I hope you're not changing your mind about your search for your birth mother, because I think I've found her." Deb went on to explain that this rapid turn of events is highly unusual and told me that what usually takes months or years and sometimes never happens seemed to be happening miraculously.

"You think you've found her?" I asked. It didn't feel real. All of the sudden I felt a rush of excitement. "Can you tell me anything about her? What is she like?"

Deb said, "I can tell you that she is very nice and all she kept saying was, "I can't believe she wanted to find me." She kept repeating that over and over again as if that was all she could say. I will also tell you her first name. "Her name is Eileen."

"Eileen," I said. "Thank you. I will get my information to you as soon as possible."

Deb reminded me to send her a copy of my driver's license and social security card to prove my identity. I was feeling hopeful, supported and thrilled. I made the copies and placed them in the mail that day.

"Eileen…Eileen…Eileen." I kept repeating her name over and over again. It was unbelievable that I knew her name. That was huge to me. I would almost have been ok with just knowing her name because it was more than I knew before and with her name I almost felt like I knew her.

Only a week later I got a call from Deb again. "I found your birthmother," she said. "She told me it's ok for you to call her and she keeps saying she can't believe you wanted to find her."

I was feeling shock, but was enthusiastic and enlivened. I thanked Deb and took a moment to process the news I had just been given. I wasn't ready to call immediately. I needed to think about what I wanted to say and prepare myself with more courage to make the actual call. Since walking helps me process big news, I went for an exuberant and exhilarating hour-long walk around my neighborhood. I thought about what I would say and wondered what my mother would be like when I called. When I returned from my walk, I sat down at the kitchen table to make the most important call of my life. I sat with a pen and notebook. I wrote down a few questions to ask her in case I froze up and didn't know what to say. I wrote down: brothers and sisters, favorite foods, favorite color and recreational activities. Then I dialed the number.

A woman picked up the phone and answered with "Hello?"

I asked, "Is this Eileen?"

She said, "Yes."

I quickly responded, "Hi, this is Stacie."

She said, "I can't believe you wanted to find me."

I said, "I am so happy I did. I have so many questions for you." I couldn't believe I was speaking to my biological mother for the first time. I was listening to the tone of her voice and was in shock and awe simultaneously. I wanted to know everything and anything. I proceeded to ask,

"Do I have any brothers or sisters?"

She replied, "You have one sister and two brothers." She told me more about them, their names, their ages and what they were doing now. I discovered she had her next child, my brother, just 14 months after me and that she raised him and my other two siblings with their father, a man she met and married shortly after she gave me up for adoption. She is still married to him today and he wanted her to change her mind about the adoption so she could keep me by not signing a second set of papers six months after the adoption. However, she had already signed the first papers and I was already with my new family. She told me that when she considered that option she couldn't do that to me and my new parents because my new parents and I would have already developed attachment and love.

I have a different father than my siblings, but she isn't sure who my father is. She said, "We will find out who your father is. The father listed on your original birth certificate was a friend of mine who agreed to be listed, and he may be your father, but there are also two other potential fathers." Wow, I thought, this is unexpected and surprising news. Now I felt like my story was becoming like the musical and movie "Mama Mia," in which the main character, Sophie, discovers her mother's diary and uncovers that she has three possible fathers.

I told my birthmother, "A week ago Deb told me your name for the first time and I kept repeating your name over and over again because I couldn't believe I finally knew your name. It was so exciting to know your name because I felt like I was closer to knowing you."

I asked her what she liked to do and what her favorite foods and colors were. She told me she was haunted by the image of me as an infant and that she had been struggling a lot over the last 18 months to find me. She explained my youngest brother had been searching for me over that period of time in order to try to help her find me. It's as if my soul heard the call of her soul. All she wanted was to know me and all she could imagine when she spoke to me was the image of me as a beautiful little infant girl with red hair. She kept seeing me the way I looked on the day we both left the hospital, the only day the nurses let her briefly see and hold me.

We were both dying to see what the other looked like and agreed to exchange photographs by mail as it was January 2001, before the convenience of mainstream photo text messaging and email. We spoke for an hour and in that hour, other than answering my questions, all she could say was, "I can't believe you wanted to find me. I was struggling so much and wanted to find you but I didn't know how. I prayed and asked for you to find me. I can't believe it actually happened."

I was suddenly awakened by the revolution that I could now actually know my biological mother. I had been waiting my entire life for this. She had been the void missing in my life for all this time and now I could finally have a relationship with her. The parts of me that were lost were beginning to be filled in and I felt like I could finally get the answers to all the questions I longed to know.

We spoke a few times over the next couple months and my mother told me something that cannot be explained by logic. One day, she reminded me of when I told her about my first learning her name and said, "A week before you called me, I was at work and I kept hearing my name being called but when I turned to look, no one was there. It felt like someone was over my left shoulder calling my name in my left ear." My mother said, "I wanted to tell you I kept hearing my name being called but I didn't want you to think I was crazy and when I heard my name being called it was exactly a week before we talked on the phone, the exact same day you found out what my name was." We couldn't believe something like this could even happen. It was beyond explanation.

Then, another profound interconnection happened that was a miracle and directly coincided with my reunion with my birthmother. Less than two weeks after I had my first conversation with my birth mother, I discovered I was pregnant with my first child and about to become a mother myself. I soon discovered I was pregnant with a daughter of my own, which connected me to my roots in a way that I never felt before. It was indescribable, magical and unbelievable to become a mother and find my mother at the same time. I was beginning to feel connected in ways I had never felt before but there were other aspects of my life that were rising to the surface as well.

Wounds will eventually want to be seen and heard. They can only be suppressed and buried temporarily and then, just the right event will create the catalyst for them to be seen.

My adoptive mother was struggling during my reunion with my birth mother. When I made my first trip to see my birth mother, my adoptive mother was hurt but understood that I needed to know medical history, or at least that's what I told her and that seemed to not hurt her. When I made the next two visits, my adoptive mother rejected me and reignited in me my core abandonment wound. She temporarily wanted nothing to do with me and wouldn't talk to me. She also made me wrong to the rest of my adoptive family and I was told by my adoptive mother, before she cut off contact, that I don't appreciate all she did for me. My adoptive mother told me she did all the hard work of raising me, changing diapers, dealing with all the difficulties and now all of a sudden my biological mother gets to sweep in an enjoy the fruits of my adoptive mom's labors. She was hurt and it came out as anger. It was upsetting to me that she didn't realize how much grief my biological mother had gone through in missing out on all of those moments in my childhood. In reality, my biological mother cried daily for three years straight immediately following our reunion, which opened the flood gates of her pain and sorrow.

On the other hand, I had a lot to learn about compassion and empathy for what my adoptive mother went through. Not being able to have her own biological children was her deepest and most impactful wound and all I needed to do was accept her completely and show her my love and gratitude. Over time my adoptive mother and I healed our relationship issues and now my bond with her is better than ever. I was blessed beyond all possibility to have been given the adoptive mother and father I was given to raise me, as well as all of my immediate and extended family. I truly was loved the same as I would have been loved if I had been born from my adoptive mother's womb. Through them, I learned so much and I realize now more than ever how lucky I am to have two families who love me.

RETURNING TO LOVE

A core belief that our culture carries is that there is only so much love to go around and that love has an end to it. We believe if we give love to one, then love toward another must be taken away. This is simply untrue. We manifest this in all core relationships, whether it be lovers, friends, or family. The truth is that there is an abundance of love, love is eternal and very real. When we open to true, unconditional love, we begin to experience the depth that love has for us.

My adoption and reunion story brought me back to the union we all share, our connection to our mothers and even greater, our connection to our Divine Mother of compassion, empathy, unconditional love, creativity, receptivity, connection and joy. I began to question:

What if God was not just a masculine figure but rather masculine and feminine in one?
What if God were both God and Goddess, united and not separate and how does that relate to the disconnection in our world today?

Is this such a radical idea? Maybe not. Isn't this what we know deeply within our core? When truth touches us, we know it on a physical and cellular memory level. We all want to feel this connection, not just to and as a human mother and daughter, but also to our Divine Mother.

Everything is born from the womb of creation, and the planet we live on is feminine in nature. As we go through so many shifts and changes in our structures and the old ways of thinking, acting and interacting, we are all beginning to long for something more. My belief is that what we are all truly longing for is our connection to the whole, which includes not only God, but also the greater balance between God and the Goddess. The Goddess is not the mother we were born to, although she may appear that way in some situations, but rather the Divine Mother of all creation and infinite possibilities.

My story reminds me of the bigger picture of the rising consciousness that connects us all. The Goddess who has been silent for centuries is now rising up, needing to be seen, heard, tasted, felt, touched and experienced. She is calling each of us forth for a Divine plan. The plan is for us to fully own our power and not fear it. She is Shakti, our invisible power that calls us forth to dance, play, create, be multi-orgasmic and not take ourselves so seriously. She is calling us.

We feel it in our bones. We are being called to step into our Divine life purpose and stand up for what we feel is important. We are being told to take care of our bodies, love ourselves unconditionally and feel our connection to everything, which comes from our Divine Mother, the Goddess and Shakti. She burns away what no longer serves us and opens the doors for renewal and opportunity. All we have to do is soften and open to her, and to the promises she holds for us, which are born from the deepest love.

IN THE BEGINNING

When you were born, you were connected to all there is. There was no separation. You were not separate from your mother, the milk in her breasts, the sound of her voice. It was all connected to you, which was all connected to the whole of the universe. You didn't believe you were separate because you didn't have beliefs. You just knew you were connected to all, because that's all there was. There was nothing else to tell you differently. The problem was, as you grew, you were trained in different beliefs and different concepts of who you were. You followed your parents' lead because that's who you had to look up to.

It wasn't like the days of old, the days of your ancestors, where you were interconnected to the community as a whole. You were not separate from anyone and all had a role in helping to raise you. What happened? You lost who you were. Not because you did anything wrong, but rather because, over time, your parents and grandparents and their parents and grandparents became disconnected from their true nature and primal instincts.

They forgot everything is alive. They forgot the stones are alive. They forgot the Earth is alive. Yet, a part of you never forgot. A part of you always knew you weren't separate. That part of you is what brought you here to read this now.

In the past, religions were formed to control and have power over the masses. They showed people there is a "God," but "He" wasn't directly accessible to us all. "God" was turned into a concept and the direct experience of the Divine, which includes both God and Goddess, both light and dark, both you and I, was taken out.

I was raised in the Catholic faith and taught lessons of a God in the sky watching over and judging all of us. I was conditioned to believe we were born sinners and that we must confess our sins to the priest in order to have a direct line to God. I was taught that if we died before we were christened by the church, we would go to hell. In the world of institutionalized religion, secrets were hidden and information was withheld. Those in power only revealed the information they wanted the "common man and woman" to hear. We were fed lies.

The way we were trained to view the world was conditioned into us. We disconnected from our bodies and we disconnected from our Source. Since our incarnation into a body, in this lifetime and the lifetimes of our ancestors for as long as history documents, we have been stuck in a place of duality. There has been a belief in good/bad, right/wrong, me/you, and separateness. This is the place of ego, otherwise known as "edging God out." This is not to make the ego the villain. Our ego is part of our personality and our inborn need to survive in this world. It is meant to keep us safe and alive.

We have been disempowered, but it's time to reclaim our power. Before the institution of religion, people connected to the spirit realm in nature. Nature was revered as a great teacher and we realized we were connected to all. We understood the wisdom of the trees, the plants, the stones, the Earth and the helping spirits. We were in awareness of the knowledge of the animals and the wisdom and interconnectedness of all things. We understood the Earth was our medicine and we were to be respectful, taking only what we needed and offering our gratitude back when we were blessed with anything, whether it was from a plant or animal.

We were once connected more intimately to our true nature and the nature of all on our planet, but then we entered a time of darkness. During the time around the fifth century AD, the Catholic Church was being led by men who feared the power women appeared to possess. Therefore, in order to have power and control over the masses, it would be appropriate to remove women of their power, turn them into possessions, and make the feminine energy that of the devil. Over time, the direct connection to Spirit, the natural world, light, beauty and magic was hidden and went underground as the Church became more and more effective toward the goal of power and money through domination. The Church was successful because it presented itself as the path to take to connect the people to God, but that was the illusion.

Behind it all was the primary intent to disconnect people from their true nature and the direct connection to both God and Goddess in one. The Divine Mother and Goddess was taken out of the equation and everything seen through the eyes of the feminine was explained by those in power as from the devil. Fear took over and what was once sacred became seen as either dark or infantile perspectives, and as such, people were directed to the church for salvation.

Control of the masses and power over the people was the purpose and the only way to do this was to disempower people. They were told priests were their only direct connection to God, a masculine and fatherly figure. Mother was seen as beneath father, but this is changing in churches today and there are many wonderful and supportive churches of all faiths now.

"A new command I give you: Love one another. As I have loved you, so you must love one another."
~Jesus Christ (John 13:34, NIV)

Wisdom is returning and there are more and more of us awakening to the truth. It is the wisdom of unconditional love, beauty, and oneness with all things. We forgot we were one with all, but now we are returning to a place of remembrance.

We have been removed from spirit and from our Source, the abundant wellspring of life within each and every one of us. We have been disconnected, but we are evolving out of it all. We are transcending the difficult periods in life and we are in the amazing magical moment now. It is opening to us; all we have to do is see.

We must learn to see with new eyes, hear with new ears and transcend the thinking mind. New opportunities are opening to us along with new ways of being.

We are transitioning out of human doing-ness into human being-ness. When we realize that just being is enough, a new world opens to us. We are on the edge of that world and it is here now. All we have to do is open to the new ways of looking at it.

If we were simply born into the place of just is-ness, would we appreciate the sacred? We are all longing to enter wholeness. We are all longing to rediscover the hidden divinity within ourselves. It is not in just some of us, it is in all of us.

There is a force within each and every one of us, beckoning us to pay attention. It is calling out to us to listen. It is saying, "Listen to the heart." It is saying, "You are a soul in a body, not a body in a soul." It is saying, "Stop the insanity of the world." It is time for us to listen. It is time for us to pay attention.

We are at a pivotal time in the evolution of human consciousness. The big question is this: Who am I? The answer to this question for many years has revolved around the labels of who we think we are, such as our career, family or social title. These labels become our identity, and when we lose one or more of those labels, we question who we are. Yet, underlying all labels is an essence that is our true essential nature. Who are you? Who am I? Who are we? The question, "Who am I?" is something we all share.

We are living in a time beyond any other time that we have ever existed as human beings on this planet. It's a catalytic time of shifts, changes and growth. The doors of consciousness are opening like they never opened before and we are waking up and becoming more aware. It is time for us to embrace the shadows within us but also to acknowledge the light. As women we are powerful. And the power that the women have is beyond the traditional way that we have had power throughout our known history. We've lived for thousands of years in a patriarchal and masculine-dominated society. Now the feminine is rising to create balance, and the masculine will, in the end, come to rise in complement to it.

Here is the Yin/Yang symbol from Chinese philosophy.

It shows complete balance between the masculine (white) and feminine (black), on equal sides with center points of the masculine in the feminine and the feminine in the masculine. The feminine is going within, receiving, moon, and correlates to the left side of the body. The masculine is pushing forward, giving, sun, and correlates to the right side of the body. When the energies of the masculine and feminine come into balance, collectively and individually, for both women and men, peace is restored because the illusion of separation no longer exists.

We live in a time of extreme shifts and changes. There is darkness and light. Both are required for creation to exist on this planet. This is duality. But we are transforming beyond the old ways of having power over one another and shifting into the new ways of creating a new world of cooperation, collaboration, compassion, empathy, purpose and love.

THE INVITATION

This is a Divine invitation to release everything that's holding you back. It's an invitation to step into your wholeness. You are Divine. You are perfect just the way you are. There is nothing about you that you have to change.

I am here to accompany you on this journey into yourself. I am here to provide structure and space to allow for your Divine unfoldment that is uniquely yours. We are all on a journey and each of our journeys are unique, yet the same.

Long ago women were fully embraced and loved for the power they carried, for their power was inclusive. When the woman of the past was allowed to be fully in her power, all thrived. Nature was respected and Earth was seen as our mother.

As a woman, you are naturally intuitive and that time is coming again. It is here now. It is time for you to fully embrace your feminine power, for when you are powerful, all benefit.

There are those who may want to keep you down because they are living in fear. They are afraid of their own safety and security. They don't understand true empowerment and are living through their false identities, or in other words, they are living through their ego.

When a woman fully steps into her power, she enlightens the world, just through her presence.

This is an invitation for you to realize you are an amazing and powerful woman, beyond your wildest dreams. This power is not in the traditional sense of "power over" for self-benefit and greed, but rather the power of you. When you fully step into and embrace your power, it is the greatest power of all. It is the power of the collective. You can influence this power in ways greater than you can imagine. Trust that everything is happening for a reason. It's all going to be ok. You are meant to shine.

THIS BOOK AS A PORTAL

This book is a portal into your personal union with the Divine Mother, your higher self and the goddess within you, which is your grace, beauty, and Shakti energy. She is holding you as you are holding her. What she holds for you is a sacred space, a space for you to enter as you are, without fear of being judged and without limitations. This is the place of unconditional love.

This book is broken into three sections: Sacred Surrender, Sacred Embodiment, and Sacred Expansion. The sections are linear for the purposes of structure within the book, but they are not linear. Instead, they are, as you heal and grow, closest to the form of an energetic spiral. You rise and fall a little but each time you rise, your ceiling is higher and you are empowered to reach heights like never before. The practices allow you an opening into the understanding that processes are not linear and all healing and life is an evolution. There is, in a sense, never an ending or a final destination, and yet there is; because ultimately, you have already arrived.

PART 1: SACRED SURRENDER

Sacred Surrender is the act of letting go of the conditions and beliefs you have been taught through the culture and family you were raised in as well as the current structures and systems in place. It is about learning to gently accept all just as it is without needing to know why. When you can accept all as it is, you release the strong hold the intense emotions have on you, which then gives you an empowered place to take action from.

PART 2: SACRED EMBODIMENT

Sacred Embodiment is the action of coming fully into your body, which is the portal for healing of body, mind and spirit. For women in particular, physical embodiment it is deeply connected to the lower three energy centers (chakras) and feminine womb space. Embodiment allows an integration of the unhealed and broken parts of you that are often unconsciously leading the way, bringing them to light and allowing for reintegration from the healing. When you are fully embodied, your soul and your body are working together as one and you stand in your personal power. You reclaim your power, "own it" and don't apologize for who you are.

PART 3: SACRED EXPANSION

Sacred Expansion is an opening into what you don't know you don't know. Whether you know it or not, you are in a state where you expand and then contract so the expansive places can be integrated toward embodiment and then back out again. Expansion includes purpose, prayer, synchronicities, miracles, angels, guides and mysticism.

Throughout this book many names are used to describe the one Divine presence, including God and Goddess. This one Divine presence is beyond all names and yet includes all names. A name gives us a place mark to understand where we are together, yet because there are so many differing beliefs around who and what "God" means and Goddess is a scary word to some, the identification with a name flattens it and makes it a concept. When we give anything or anyone a name, we suddenly believe we know who they are, which takes away the curiosity, mystery, and keeps us stuck in the limited belief that something is a static or unchangeable. Change is the only thing that you can count on. Therefore, as you read this book, open your mind to any and all possibilities and also believe only what resonates with you. When it is truth, you will know it.

The tools and advice you will find among these pages are very practical, driven from the wisdom of my many years of suffering, where I didn't trust and I just feared. I wrote this book for you, my soul mate reader. If I can give you an entry into the peace that surmounts all understanding without you having to go through the degrees of suffering I have, my job is done. I realize now that my suffering was mostly self-imposed, not because I liked suffering but because I was my own worst enemy. I wanted to play the victim and blame others for my circumstances. My actions were unconscious, not coming from the conscious mind where I was aware of how I was sabotaging myself, but rather from the subconscious mind of wounds and broken parts of myself that I didn't yet fully understand or identify. I am here to accompany you on your unique journey, the one you have traveled and have still to travel. I humbly invite you to learn from the wisdom I have learned through much suffering, in the hope that some of this knowledge and wisdom can help guide your path and reduce your suffering. We are all in this together on this human and Divine sacred journey of life.

"Believe nothing, no matter where you read it or who has said it, not even if I have said it, unless it agrees with your own reason and your own common sense."
~Buddha

Stacie Ivey

PART 1

Sacred Surrender

"They tried to bury us. They didn't know we were seeds."
~Mexican Proverb

Stacie Ivey

*It brushes up against me like a feather on the skin, touching
so delicately, but I ignore it.*

"That was nothing," says my mind, so I go on with my life.

Seconds turn into minutes. Minutes turn into hours.

Hours turn into days. Days turn into months.

Months turn into seasons. Seasons turn into years.

Years and years go by until there is nothing left to me.

I am an expression of the physical world, but it is not me.

Who is it an expression of? Who wanted this?

Society?

Me?

Why?

*I was miserable. My misery sucked the core out of my being.
It made me depressed, which told me something was wrong
with the way I was living my life.*

*Something had to change. There was no more, "That's not for
me. That's for other people, not me." Putting my dreams off
until the future could no longer wait.*

*I could no longer stand by and let my life pass by me. I could
no longer just make a living for the sake of making a living.
If I didn't have a passion for it, I could no longer do it. I
could no longer wait.*

The time is now.

Surrender is the act of letting go. It is an internal cleansing of the conditioning we received within the culture we grew up in (family, state, country, religion, or gender) that leads us to create an identity from and develop roles in that we buy into with such totality that we don't see anything else. It is so deeply ingrained in us, led by the subconscious that the conscious mind is "asleep" to our external influences.

The process of sacred surrender is a shedding of the aspects of the false self, like a snake sheds it's skin or the peeling away of an onion bit by bit, and gradually going deeper into the sacred wisdom that is held within our soul for which our body is a vessel. It is an identification of the parts of us we have claimed as truth that we later realize is a false truth that arose from this conditioning. At a certain point we realize our beliefs may not be ours but rather the beliefs of our parents, teachers or culture. When we identify these beliefs no longer serve our highest and best interests, we seek something different. A transition occurs from the identification with the small self (name, body, role, car, house, career, image) into an expanded awareness the larger Divine Self, which is held in the heart and our true essence and being.

Ask yourself, "Who am I?" and open to a space of inquiry that comes from a place of curiosity. Don't prejudge. Allow for spacious awareness to come in.

Who you are is infinite, perfect, complete, connected, loved and one with all. The more you practice quieting the mind and going within, you begin to awaken through your own internal experience from which truth and wisdom arise. When you open to all possibilities, the more magical and aware you become in your own life experience.

True surrender begins with an acceptance that everything that has happened can't be changed. It is a decision to stop the "should haves," "would haves" and "could haves," and a giving up of needing to know why things happened they way they did. This is a starting point. When we can accept the past as it occurred, healing can begin.

Many times we block ourselves from the kind of healing that takes place from true surrender because we are afraid of letting our position go because we believe we are right and the other person or people were wrong, but it's a double-edged sword. While we think we're protecting ourselves, holding onto to the pain, anger and resentment is just a trick of the ego. The ego wants to step in and say "I'm right," or "I'm justified in what I think." The ego wants to be heard and thinks it's more important than anything else. Remember, the ego is nothing more than the part of us that helps keep us safe in the world. It's not good or bad, it just is. The problem with the ego is when all identification gets lost within the shell of the ego; there is no room for miracles, blessings, joy and true love.

Surrender is life's invitation to step away from our ego's need to control and keep us safe and transition to a place of allowance. It is a shift from thinking and doing to just being. As we open to receive rather than forcing everything to happen, we open to miracles unfolding naturally in our lives.

Growing up, allowing myself to just be wasn't easy for me. I felt I had to achieve, succeed, think and do to accomplish a certain career, status, and family life in order to be happy. Over time, I began to realize external circumstances aren't what create true happiness and the answer became to go within, but not before going through a tremendous amount of suffering. Facing this caused me to take a look at my priorities and what I really wanted in my life.

My life has been filled with whispers that I didn't hear, knocks that I chose to ignore, tornadoes that made me start to pay attention, and earthquakes that were my wake-up calls. I have seen life as an unfolding of me. I have been the onion, peeling away the layers of my illusions and the snake shedding her skin to transform into another level of awareness. I have learned the disasters that arise from a place of resistance to what is and the traumas that happen, over and over again, when I have been unwilling or unable to release my attachment to people, places or things.

Throughout my struggles, I have learned that the more I think I know, the less I actually know. I have been turned inside out and upside down to come face to face with the God I thought I knew in childhood, only to realize everything I thought I knew was an illusion. Yet as a child I also knew and connected to something deeper, something more magical and real, as all children do. I have learned to turn to deeper and more mystical truths by going within through studying meditation, learning yoga and exploring many spiritual teachings and paths.

I grew up believing in a utopian world, where goodness and all things were possible. I believed in collaboration, compassion, empathy, trust, faith, and love. I believed in magic, unicorns, fairies, mermaids, beauty and the in the possibilities in all of mankind. I believed that we could live as people, together in unity and collaboration where goodness resides and all flourish.

Yet I came into this life during a time when all of it was reaching a peak. The world we live in has been lost in desire for power and control, resulting in overconsumption, violence, greed, and self-serving desires, but this will change because it is not sustainable.

We are the ones we have been waiting for. We can change this path toward destruction and turn the ship around when we set our differences aside, create balance and come together as one.

CHAPTER 1

SURRENDERING INTO THE FEMININE

"I am a human being, not a human doing."
~Kurt Vonnegut

We are living in an out-of-balance world focused on productivity. As a result, we have become out of balance and sick. The western world is a culture of production. We are told we must produce, achieve, be successful and reach perfection all in one. Our worthiness is determined by what is outside of us, such as our career, house, car or partner and our identity is caught up in what we own. This leads to comparison and competition and can take us to an extreme place of living, where enough is never enough.

We are told that if we don't conform to society's or our family's expectations of the career we must have, we face the real fear of judgment and lack of acceptance by our tribe. This is what we believe and whether we'd like to admit it or not, this is what we are taught. This is not to say that producing and creating is a bad thing. It's just out of balance. We have created a culture of beliefs and then rules and laws around those beliefs. We are entrenched in a pile of garbage beliefs. We are at the garbage dump buried under layers and layers of trash.

There is a way out. That path is taking one moment at a time and questioning, "Does that belief system serve my highest and best interest?" It is an appropriate question and can seem like a radical idea at first because we aren't taught to question this. We are taught to be sheep. There have always been the few who have questioned the status quo. They are the change makers, the ones who were seen as extremists at the time, but they have always been there and we need them.

As women, it is time for us to learn to receive. It is time for us to stop being so hard and get soft. Getting soft doesn't mean to have no boundaries and let others walk all over you. Rather, softening means surrendering to the feminine essence that is you. It is surrender into the beauty and love that is within and has never left you. It is a return to what it truly means to be a woman.

It is time for all of us to begin to question the situations we find ourselves in, not just in the world, but starting within our own beliefs, thoughts and lives first. I have found as I uncover my own beliefs and thoughts, realizing they are not me and that I have been conditioned a certain way, it is crazy how the real truth rises out of all the muck. In yoga, the visual of the lotus flower rising up from the muck and mud into a beautiful flower is used as a lesson for how a human being can rise out of the collective conditioned consciousness into the consciousness of the higher self, the God self, the Source within us all. Jesus said, "Even the least among you can do what I have done and greater things;" (John 14:12) and Christianity teaches, "You are a child of God." (Psalm 139)

It is time for us to step out of the belief that God is a condemning and judging God who wants us to be a certain way, which involves conforming to a certain mold. When we open to leaving that outdated story of God, we open to a more compassionate and forgiving God. As we open, we embrace all and have compassion for all human suffering.

This is when we open to both God and Goddess, for she is God in feminine form.

She is the aspect of God that was suppressed and lost.

She is nurturing and unconditionally loving and she wants us to be who we are in the rawest and most authentic way possible.

She is Shakti.

She is the creative life force.

She is beauty.

She is life.

We fear becoming our most authentic selves because we were conditioned to play small, but when we become who we truly are, our authentic Divine essence, it is intoxicating. We become a light onto the world. It doesn't mean we never have challenges. Life is full of them, but the more we grow, the stronger we become and we learn what is really important in life. It becomes really clear.

As I became more and more conditioned by my family and culture, I became a human doing. I forgot what it was to be a human being. I got further lost and detached from who I was. I was so arrogant and self-centered. I didn't pay attention to the people and things around me. I lost my way.

I love the song, "Amazing Grace," because it perfectly explains the process the songwriter was going through when he discovered the truth, the truth of who he was. His journey was very humbling and a true experience of coming back to being a human being. Just being alive is enough. When I understood this, it was a profound shift for me. It was a shift that had a tremendous ripple effect. I realized the Divine is beyond what our minds can understand but is available to us at any moment, any time. All we have to do is ask.

Invitation: *Ask yourself, "What if my just being was enough?"*

THE FEMININE SIDE OF THE BRAIN

*"I am the right brain. I am creativity. A free spirit. I am passion.
Yearning. Sensuality. I am the sound of roaring laughter. I am taste. The
feeling of sand beneath bare feet. I am movement. Vivid colors. I am
the urge to paint on an empty canvas. I am boundless imagination. Art.
Poetry. I sense. I feel. I am everything I wanted to be. "*
~Author Unknown

We have two hemispheres in our brain. Each hemisphere of the brain correlates with the opposite side of the body. The left hemisphere/right body is based in logic, reasoning, linear thinking, force, drive, and productivity. It is the energy of the sun and the space or container that holds all things. It is the energy of the masculine, which is within all of us, whether we are male or female. It wants to be right and it likes to keep you safe and protected. It is good at order, math and language processing, to name a few.

The right hemisphere/left body houses intuition, creativity, art, music, dance, empathy, compassion and non-linear reality. It is the energy of the feminine and it is also within all of us. The right hemisphere is responsible for unity, connection and creativity.

In the collective brain, culturally and worldly, at this time in history, we are operating on a more left-brained, masculine energy. This is the energy of the universe that created our buildings and roads, structures, laws, rules and routines. It has been necessary and is good. Yet, there has been an imbalance of the feminine, right side of the brain, which is focused on love and is beauty in the world. Our feminine side creates our appreciation of beautiful things, our craving to be creative and our desire to love, nurture, and care for others.

RETURNING TO BALANCE

"Western women will save the world."
~The Dalai Lama

There is a balance that is currently missing in our world today. It is the balance between the masculine and feminine aspects of the Divine Mother and Father God, Goddess, the Holy Spirit, the Tao, Allah, universe or whatever name we choose to call the One Source of all.

We live in a world that has been dominated by the masculine for far too long and we are seeing the dire effects of that over-domination today. We are seeing crisis on the individual and global levels. Never before have we as a human species and planet been so out of balance.

Imagine the scales, where if you place equal weight between the two, you create balance and equality. The same is true with the Chinese yin/yang symbol. There is an equal balance between the two, yet there are aspects of each in the other. Masculine in the symbol is represented by the color white (sun, outward energy, giving) and feminine is represented by the color black (moon, inward energy, receiving). In the list on the next page are examples of left-brain (masculine) and right-brain (feminine) energy.

Masculine Energy	Feminine Energy
Doing	Being
Thinking/reasoning	Creating
Pushing forward/force	Allowing
Outward-looking	Inward-looking
Outer authority	Inner authority
Analyzing	Sensing
Making decisions	Using intuition
Giving	Receiving
Single-pointed focus	Gestalt or big picture
Black and white	Spectrum of color
Logic (Limited to 5 Senses)	Beyond logic
Mind	Body
Practical/rational	All-encompassing
Direct	Indirect
Words	Images
Linear	Circles and spirals
Separate	Whole
Limited	Unlimited
Power forward	Power within
Passion	Sensuality
Reasoning	Empathy
Stability	Flow
Aggressive	Passive
Confidence	Radiance
Independence	Collaboration
Non-emotional	Emotional
Yang/White	Yin/Black
Sun	Moon

The way this manifests in our world today is through our beliefs, where fear and separateness rule over love and wholeness. Caroline Myss discovered four primary archetypes in her work as a medical intuitive that every individual carries, as outlined in her book, *Sacred Contracts*, which include the victim, saboteur, child, and prostitute. Based on my humble understanding of these primary archetypes as well as a few others I have seen and experienced, some examples include:

- My beliefs are right and yours are wrong.
- There is not enough (time, money, resources), so I need to fight for mine.
- The body is compartmental and separate from the whole (including mind and spirit).

What is missing in our world today is the feminine being in equal balance with the masculine. She is the feminine face of God, our Divine Mother. She is the Mother to all of us, the one Mother who encompasses all mothers, all Goddesses and the Divine Feminine. She is within every woman and is also within every man.

What is the Divine Feminine?

God or the Divine is neither male nor female, but both. The Divine Feminine is life, compassionate awareness, unconditional love, intuition, feminine power and juicy, creative Shakti energy. Through her beauty and grace, pouring out of us is creative expression of all kinds, including inspired writing, music, art, dance and love. She is form held within formlessness, the space of creation of God. God holds the space for the Goddess to play and create. In the form of Goddess Kali, She is the destroyer of what is false in order for us to step into our true, Divine, authentic selves.

The Divine Feminine is flow, healing, nurturing, receptivity, sensuality, harmony, connection, the moon, forgiveness, wisdom, birth, renewal, embodiment and restoration. She is everything in and of the right hemisphere of our brains and beyond.

Stacie Ivey

THE PROCESS OF SEEKING AND DISCOVERY

"What you seek is seeking you."
~Rumi

We are all looking for a deeper meaning in life, whether we realize it or not. Sometimes the deeper meaning finds us through an unexpected event; a trauma of some sort, like a divorce or a disease. Trauma can be our greatest teacher. Its purpose is to bring us closer to our source.

There is an inner wisdom within all of us that is guiding us to the truth. It is guiding us beyond suffering. It is guiding us to love. The problem is that we don't trust it. We don't know what it is. We feel we have to stay in control to be protected.

Actually, the opposite is true. The more you cling to things, the more people and things in your life will fall away, until you begin to notice that those things aren't the true nature of happiness. The things of this world cannot make you fully happy because they are superficial. Letting go of superficiality and being willing to go deeper is what opens you to the truth. It opens you to love, and love is the only thing that's real. Love is all there is. Everything comes from love.

What you seek is actually seeking you. It is your own inner wisdom. It is the instinct you were born with. It is the truth of who you are. It is God, Goddess, the universe, the Source of and the everlasting, unconditional love that is within and of all.

When God and Goddess become revealed from within, we realize they are one in the same and we are one with them. At the deepest levels of truth, there is no separation, only oneness, wholeness and unity. This discovery evokes the deepest aspects of our true nature as the layers of who we think we are and were peel away one by one.

THE TRANSITION FROM CONCEPT TO DIRECT EXPERIENCE WITH THE DIVINE

"Refuse to be content with just the knowledge of God, but insist on experiencing His presence."
~Kerri Weems

When we transition from the conceptual understanding of God that most of us have been raised with, we open to the sacred in ways beyond our wildest imagination. Direct experience with the Divine turns our understanding of God from a flat concept to an embodied, profound, sensual, exploratory, joyous and profound grace that appears as a gift when we are open and ready. The more we focus on directing our understanding of God to wanting to experience God, the more we begin to live, see, feel, taste, smell and touch the world and everything in it as God.

The experience of "God" is the experience as both the beloved and lover. It is the God who cannot be named because no name can describe Her and Him. God is the consciousness beyond and within all living and nonliving things within both form and formlessness. God/Goddess is the masculine and feminine in one. It is the overarching awareness that we all have within our bodies as well as the breath that is breathing us. It is the intelligence and creativity that has brought all things into being and is all. At the level of God, there is no separation, only unity.

When we begin to understand the greater God, which is beyond the understanding of the brain, we learn of grace, miracles and the bridge to the sacred. We don't understand what we haven't experienced. Our religions have mostly taught us of a God that is outside of us. As a child who grew up Catholic, I was taught that God was up in the clouds

37

watching over us, judging us, and was just beyond our reach because we were born sinners and the only way to connect with God was through prayer and confessing our sins to a priest. The prayer component was the piece that allowed a more intimate connection with God. But I never felt I really understood what prayer was for, other than to ask God for help, which usually meant to take away suffering of some sort or another. This I agree with, but there is so much more to prayer. I believe our understanding of God is limited to the teachings we were exposed to as children. We didn't know what we didn't know. Now, with all of the information on the Internet, in magazines, and on television, we have access to a bigger picture, more voices, and the ability to question what we believe or don't believe.

When God is out of reach, we feel disempowered, lost and alone. We feel like God is outside of us and we seek pleasure and joy from things outside of us. When we believe God is judging us, we judge each other and ourselves, and then we create systems of judgment. As children, our parents and then our teachers judge us. We fear our principals. Then, as we get older, we fear the law and police. We are conditioned to be "good" because we ultimately don't believe we are good inside because we are taught we are born as sinners.

Our court system, for example, is a system of judgment. The judge acts as "God" and the individuals on both sides play out strategies in order to "win." Our legal system was originally set up to be fair and to protect all but because greed and corruption exist, it frequently isn't fair Many individuals working for and of power within the system also make a lot of money off of people fighting in court. It's like there is a fire and the attorneys (some not all) take kerosene and add it to the fire to keep it going. Often, the people in power and with more money and connections are in control and in turn, get what they want. It is about winning and is often the same with politics as well. Many of us allow the dysfunctional systems to continue because the problem seems too big and we don't know the first thing to do to make a positive change. Many times we don't speak up because we have felt so disempowered and we don't know where to begin. Yet, when we come together and take small and empowered steps, change can happen.

When we understand the true nature of the Divine, we recognize that everything is connected, everything is sacred, and the masculine and feminine are both beautiful and meant to be in balance. We see the connection between all of nature and ourselves. We get back in touch with our animal selves and have deep and profound respect for the cycles of life and the gifts that are bestowed upon us.

Collectively and subconsciously, we carry beliefs with us that serve to create our actions in the world. As a majority, we currently believe in more in lack than abundance, yet when we look around, there is more abundance than there ever has been in the history of our civilization. It is time for us to let go of poverty consciousness, survival consciousness, victim consciousness and many other number of beliefs that are keeping us stuck in fear. Awareness and healing are the way to begin releasing these beliefs that no longer serve us or humanity as a whole, as well as our planet and every living thing on it.

Stacie Ivey

CHAPTER 2

HEALING THE PRIMAL WOUND

It taps, it knocks, it whispers, it yells, it screams, patiently, silently waiting until you listen. "I will wait for you as long as it takes," a voice whispers "until you see that you must let go. You must release the security blanket that is holding you back."

Today I see this: The primal scream has been tugging at me, preparing me, and releasing me from the false sense of security of my job. It has been trying to tell me all along that I don't need to keep seeking and thinking I don't have enough. I have to trust and believe I have all that I need and more, but it really sucks trying to trust and believe when I don't see it yet. How can I believe it's coming?

When we can't take it anymore, our soul lets out a primal scream. It arises, bellows, and falls. It comes from the deepest and darkest parts of us, connecting deep into the core of the Earth and then rises up like a volcano from the center of the lava pool at the deepest center of our being.

It is a crying out to be heard. It cannot be held in any longer and the only option is to let it go. The act of letting go is another form of death, not the physical death of the body, as we usually associate with death, but the death of the self that isn't real. It is the death of the part of us that believed we were anything other than love. It's the death of the roles, the abuses, the anger, the fear, and the playing small. It's the death of being controlled by anything other than our highest self and letting it all go.

We want to be heard. We want to be seen and loved for who we truly are, which is Divine. We want to be acknowledged. Yet there is within us a part that is showing us what needs to be revealed in order to hear what isn't being heard, seen or acknowledged. That is the part we need to pay attention to.

Where is it coming from? What person isn't showing up for us or giving us what we need? When we seek for pleasure, joy and satisfaction outside of ourselves, we are always disappointed. Maybe not at first and maybe not in every situation, but over time, it is inevitable. Why? Because when we seek from a place of "out there" and not "in here," we are left with loss, fear, unworthiness and a lack of deep satisfaction. When we transition to going within and working through all the blocked areas that are held in our minds, bodies, and psyches, we can then heal the unhealed wounds.

__Invitation:__ Let it go. Scream. If you aren't in touch with who you really are and feel a deep sense of aching inside, let it all go. All that matters is that you are willing to dive within and get curious. It's about a deeper inquiry into yourself and the wisdom of your soul, your higher Self, your God or Goddess self, or whatever name to choose to call the truth of who you are, which is Divine.

THE DARK NIGHT OF THE SOUL

"In the dark night of the soul, bright flows the river of God."
~St. John of the Cross

The dark night of the soul is a death, not of the body, but rather of a false sense of identity or fear based belief system with which we have become attached. It is not an actual physical death, although it feels like a physical death. Even though we don't physically die, we feel like we want to. It brings us to our knees and our skin feels like it's crawling. In the moment of the dark night of the soul we want to escape the pain, but the pain is so unbelievable and excruciating, we don't know what to do but to drop to our knees and cry from the deepest and darkest parts of our being. Our soul is crying out for its truth to be heard. The crying isn't normal crying. It is the deep wailing that feels like it's coming from the depths of our soul. In the moment of the dark night of the soul, we feel powerless, helpless and afraid. We feel like giving up, and yet at that exact moment, there is a calling from within that we may in actuality hear for the first time. It is the calling of our soul. It is the calling of God/Goddess.

I have experienced two separate occasions where I had a dark night of the soul. One was during the time of my divorce and the second was during the time of a extended physical separation from my own children. Both caused me to question everything and both brought me to my knees into a deep wailing cry which felt similar to giving birth as I was no longer in control. The only way out of the pain I felt was to completely surrender. I cried to the point of being a puddle on the floor and prayed. Then a miracle occurred and the weight was lifted from me. I relaxed into a rebirthing of me in a different form. I still looked the same but was transformed from within for the better. Going through it also made me face my fear of death and when I came out on the other side, I realized I was stronger than I thought I was.

During the dark night of the soul, we are presented with the choice of surrender to the experience of it and it feels like a death because a wounded part of us dies. We want out and will accept anything that will relieve us of the pain and discomfort. When we choose to just let go, and it may not even be an actual choice but rather your higher self taking over because it is like going through physical labor pains, afterward the experience is a peace and a grace that comes in that overrides it all, and is beyond all understanding. It makes no sense to the logical mind because everything else shuts down and a portal opens into a direct experience with the Divine.

When we surrender to the dark night of the soul, we are having a felt, intimate, direct experience with the Divine. It may be the first Divine experience we remember in a long time because we have forgotten who we are. It's not an easy path. In fact, it's f---ing hard, but it's worth it because we are never the same after and will never forget the experience. It becomes a cellular memory and takes us into a higher level of awakening out of the sleep state; the dream world of illusion that we think is real. It is profound and awe-inspiring.

The dark night of the soul is the complete loss of control and the only possible release is to drop to our knees and cry. Cry it all out. Let it all go. It is the release that is needed to open us to who we really are. We are all children of the Divine and that will never change. It is the only truth that is real. We are pure, unconditional love.

The dark night of the soul is a transition and a clearing of the part of us that isn't real and ultimately it is nothing to fear. It is the death of the part of us that thinks we are separate from God. It is the peeling away of the onion, layer by layer. If it appears, it is essential for our spiritual growth. It is the language of the soul, the crying out.

In the dark night of the soul, the only way out is in. The only way to the light is through the darkness. We are tempted to want to escape the world because to be in the world feels so excruciating. It feels so painful, that the only thing we can do is cry out to our Divine Mother and Father God, because in that moment, we realize we are not in control.

It is a death and a birth in one. It is the transition from the ego being front and center to taking a back seat, which can feel like a death because the ego is used to being the primary one in charge. Giving the ego a presence and allowance, but knowing it is not our true Self is key. The moment that feels like a death, simultaneously an opening occurs. This is the opening to the birthing of our authentic or true Self. It is the Self we are and have always been. Death is necessary for rebirth. It is the cycle, just like the leaves must change color and fall off the trees in autumn, so must we change color and fall to experience our true rebirth.

Invitation: Consider that we live in a world of duality, of darkness and light. We believe based on our conditioning, from family, culture and friends. We have lived for thousands of years in darkness and light. This is a time in our evolution of great change. The darkness is becoming more and more exposed and when the light shines on the darkness, it has nowhere to hide. When it can no longer hide, it is able to be seen and released. When it stays in the darkness, it hides, but it doesn't go away. It will show itself through multiple unconscious patterns that repeat over and over again until they can be seen.

Anything that is dark is ultimately not to be feared. It is simply in the dark because we don't see it or we are afraid to see it. When we release our fears, we begin to open more and more to light and realize that the light is real. If we lit a small candle in a pitch black room, what would we see? The light.

WHEN TRAUMA, SHOCK, AND LOSS HAPPEN

"When traumas, be they extreme or mild, are not resolved they leave behind a slew of painful, unprocessed feelings in the unconscious. These feelings are never content to remain silent and instead clamor for release. When they express themselves openly and without disguise this activates the healing process."
~Daniel Mackler

In the nature of healing, it is loss that is often the opening into the new beginning. We are offered an opportunity to open the door to a level of strength and peace we never knew we had. The doorway can be through a trauma, tragedy or disease. Once you enter the door, you never come back the same. It is the wakeup call that stops us in our tracks. It is the thing that says, "I will not be ignored any longer. I need to be seen. I need to be heard. I need to be paid attention to. You can't pretend any longer. You can't continue on your current path, not because you're being punished, but because your current path is not good for you."

This message is stated perfectly by author Kris Carr, who said, "I was asleep at the wheel before cancer shook me awake." When presented with the unexpected in a way that stops us in our tracks, we are given the opportunity to open and awaken in a way we never would have without that event.

Throughout my life, I have experienced many traumas, beginning as early as in utero, with my birthmother feeling anxiety, pain and anguish over knowing she wouldn't be able to keep me. The minute I was born, the nurses took me from my mother, not allowing her to hold me. I bonded with her in utero, and my soul knew her soul. This single event was pivotal in my life, creating deep psychic wounds and scars, which led to the key choices and decisions I made throughout my life, though at the time I never realized it. I didn't realize

I was being led by my subconscious. I didn't understand the impact of what every adult around me during my childhood considered to be a situation that would have little to no impact on me. The realization didn't come to me until much later.

Tool: I recommend using Emotional Freedom Technique, which involves self-tapping the meridian points of the body with your fingertips while saying a scripted dialogue. It helps to watch a video of it being done. Many videos are free and online. Google EFT for whatever your pain is, such as physical pain, emotional pain, or mental pain. It helps you release old beliefs and patterns.

SHINING A LIGHT ON THE DARKNESS

"All negativity is caused by an accumulation of psychological time and denial of the present. Unease, anxiety, tension, stress worry-all forms of fear-are caused by too much future and not enough presence. Guilt, regret, resentment, grievances, sadness, bitterness and all forms of non-forgiveness are caused by too much past and not enough presence."
~Eckhart Tolle

Let yourself hurt.
Let yourself be angry.
Let it all come out.

We must go through the darkness to open to the light. It is paradoxical, but true. Look at the way we usually heal a cut on our skin. We place it into darkness by covering it with a bandage in order to allow the work to be done beneath the surface.

Similarly, we fear what we don't understand and we are often afraid of what's beneath our own surfaces of image and illusion we have created for the world to see. When we are suffering and wanting out of suffering, the only way out is through. We want the quick escape plan, the drive-through-fast-food-delivery model. We want instant gratification, but it doesn't work that way. The only way out of suffering is through the suffering.

Some suffering is emotional and some is physical. Depending on the issue, either can be excruciatingly painful.

A physical suffering I experienced that took me through the darkness and into the light was the birth of my daughter. On the day of my daughter's birth, I woke up at 1:15 am to go to the bathroom. On the way to the bathroom, my water broke. I thought I would get an epidural to take away any pain from labor and delivery. My labor pains kept getting more and more intense. All I was doing was begging for the doctor to come and give me an epidural. There was only one anesthesiologist in the hospital and she was tied up with an emergency C-section. I waited and my labor increased. It got so intense that the only way I could endure the pain was to push through the contractions when they came. My body took over and I completely surrendered to the experience. In that moment, I began to feel like I was having an out of body experience, yet I was still in my body. The doctor finally arrived and when the nurses got me quickly set up, she told me to push through the next contraction. It only took two contractions and mostly involuntary pushing for my daughter to be born.

Through this experience I learned we aren't as in control as we think we are. We are truly one with the wholeness of the universe. We are all connected in such a beautiful and intricate way that we can't fully understand at the human level. Yet, at the level of Spirit, we can.

What if we allowed ourselves to fully feel so that we could release? When we avoid, the darkness stays as stuck energy in our bodies. We fear strong emotions, yet emotions are simply "energy in motion." We have a lot of judgment around emotions, but they are simple physics. We are told that it's ok to have positive emotions but not negative ones. In order to fit in, we learn to hold back the negative feelings that arise in us because these feelings make us or others feel uncomfortable. We have been conditioned this way, and it is also innate in our survival to choose pleasure over pain. Even the identification with and labeling of positive emotions versus negative emotions is conditioning. The problem with this approach is that when we don't allow ourselves to authentically feel all of our feelings, just as we are feeling them, they get stuffed in some way or another in the body. We overeat, drink too much or develop addictions. Over time, what we are avoiding comes out as rage or disease.

It seems paradoxical because when we are hurting we want to avoid the pain, but instead, we really need to allow all the feelings to come through us. It is only when we allow the crying to happen, the anger to come out, that release takes place. Only then can we truly begin to heal.

Invitation: *What feelings have you been holding back that you need to release? What would be a healthy way to release them? Consider letting them out through journaling, art, a walk, talking to a trusted friend or advisor, crying or a good scream, yoga, or going to a martial arts or self defense class.*

Stacie Ivey

ENTERING THE PRESENT MOMENT

"The present moment is the only moment available to us, and it is the door to all moments."

~Thich Nhat Hanh

When we are caught in big suffering, one of the best tools available to us at any time is to stay present. The present moment is where life is. There is no other moment but the present moment. Staying with the present moment means staying with the breath, each inhale as we inhale and each exhale as we exhale. It is that simple. Next is feeling our physical bodies. Our bodies are where the present moment lives. When we stay connected to our physical body, it is a portal to the present moment and it is a constant.

Most of my life I resisted the present moment. I have always been very caught in my thoughts. I lamented about the past. Actually, lamented is an understatement. I lived the past over and over, cycling through stories, guilt, shame and remorse, over and over. It kept me locked in trauma, which created drama and affected all aspects of my present. I was being taken down with each wave of thoughts that entered my mind, and each one crushed me into hours of tears and crashing waves of emotion. I felt like my body had been beaten up and I continued the torture onto myself for years, thinking that it would just go away on its own. I thought I could think my way out of it, but my subconscious kept bringing the trauma back up and out, over and over again until I had enough.

I knew I was either going to transform this self-imposed addiction to the past, or I would die. I had to choose. I had placated it for as long as I possibly could, and a huge wakeup call came in and said, "It's now time." If you don't do this now, you are going to destroy everything you have. I was so sick of myself, and my body couldn't handle it anymore. I didn't want to live. I wanted to die, especially in the moments when the pain was so intense, so unbearable. It is in those moments, I have found, you either fall to your knees and beg for some relief from the pain or you kill yourself. Thankfully, I chose the prior. At that moment is when grace comes in.

Grace is described as a peace that surmounts all understanding, because it does. It's the only way to describe it because the mind can't comprehend it. It is beyond the mind's ability to understand. Grace is indescribable in the world, because it is not of this world. Grace is the gift of the Goddess, coming in to support and love you, unconditionally, when you aren't able to do so yourself.

Invitation: *Breathe in. Feel your breath as it enters your body. Feel your belly rise. Breathe out. Feel your breath as it leaves your body. Feel your belly fall. Try this practice again and again. Connect to your breath. Your breath lives in the present moment, as does your body.*

As an alternative, consider going into nature or even connect with a plant. Nature contains the same vibrational frequency as your body. That is why it is calming. Nature is another portal into the present moment. The present moment is all there is. Our minds tell us differently, but the past and future are only in the present moment.

Then, go back to your breath. Your breath is one of the easiest ways to freely enter the present moment at any time. It can be done anywhere and at anytime. All it takes is attention, awareness and practice.

Stacie Ivey

CHAPTER 3

LETTING GO

"Sometimes letting things go is an act of far greater power than defending or hanging on."
~Eckhart Tolle

Letting go comes when we begin to realize that we aren't as in control as we think we are. When we reach the point of no return, we must surrender. Sometimes the act of surrender feels like death, but it isn't a death to fear. It is not a physical death, but rather a spiritual one. Letting go is learning to trust that there is something greater than the identity we have all been conditioned to believe in, the identity that is of the ego, separation, conditioning and isolation. It's the part of us that believes we aren't good enough or whole just as we are. It's the part of us that bought into the story that we had to conform or change in order to fit the mold of what society expected of us as women. Letting go is the act of laying it all down and letting it go. Some things never belonged to us and we believed they did because that's what we were told. Now it's time to let it all go.

STEP 1: THE BEGINNINGS OF SURRENDER

"To be broken is no reason to see all things as broken."
~Mark Nepo

Surrender is the act of letting go, not just once, but over and over again, as if peeling away the layers of an onion one by one. Surrender is necessary when we hit a certain point in life where what once worked no longer works. This comes from deep within our soul, asking us to listen to what's not serving our highest and best interest.

Often the beginning of true surrender is preceded by a traumatic event. The reason it happens this way is because we often don't question things when life is easy. If we were never challenged, we would never experience the dimensions of our human experience, which includes all the range of emotions. This is part of the depth of the human experience, so experience all, both light and dark to see what is real. If only the light existed, we would never appreciate it in the way that we can because of the duality that exists. Duality shows us everything about the human experience. As we grow and evolve through our experiences, we begin to understand the bigger picture and then we can let go of the judgments we used to carry about people and situations. This is not to say what happens in the world is ok, good or just, because many horrific atrocities happen. Rather, when we can step out of judgment, we are abler to take inspired action in a way that benefits all.

When we let go, we let go of needing to know why things happen the way they do. We understand that we may never know the eagle-view perspective of the situation. The ability to see above the trees when you are in the middle of the forest is a gift of grace and it usually takes time. It takes spaciousness and comes from a practice of care, love and compassion for ourselves.

True surrender is a letting go of the analysis paralysis of the mind. We forgive others and ourselves from a place of compassion, at whatever degree we are able to at that time. The more we can surrender the more freedom we feel. This may be just starting with the willingness to say you aren't ready to forgive and may never be, but are open to the possibility of someday that changing within us.

LAYING YOUR BURDENS DOWN

"Take the gentle path."
~George Herbert

Life is messy. When we are struggling, we are in a place of deep and profound suffering and there doesn't seem to be a way out. We don't know what to do. We are attached to our stories, roles, the actions of others, and our cultural conditioning. When we believe we are those things, we are stuck in a place of fear and loss, and this can continue in a looping pattern until we decide it's time for something different. We hit a point that we can't take it anymore and we have a choice at that moment. In that moment, we may take the road of giving up, at least for a time, and take ourselves out of the world through drugs, detachment or worse. Or, we may choose to "let go and let God."

When we make the second choice, a freedom arises and a weight is lifted off. We learn we can't do it anymore on our own and reach for a higher power, even if we don't fully believe or understand what a higher power, Source, or God is at that time. We just let go because letting go is the only option that our soul is allowing us to make. In the choice of letting go, we are able to begin the process of healing, of release, of forgiveness and surrender. A shedding of our skin begins to happen, and profound and unexplainable synchronicities begin to appear.

Surrender the guilt, shame, and judgments. Surrender the fear and lack of accomplishment. Surrender the fact that you think you are too old, or fat or dumb to do something great. Surrender all the thoughts, beliefs and people who tell you that you can't do it. Surrender it all.

Invitation: Follow this guided meditation. You can read it and then do the practice or have someone read it to you. Close your eyes.

Imagine a strong, heavy, wooden table of great substance standing in front of you. It is a table made especially for you. It is strong, sturdy, and can hold anything. The table is in front of you.

What does it look like?

What is it made of?

What color is it?

What do you notice about this table?

When you have an image in front of you, think of whatever is bothering you most.

Imagine you can give this table all of your burdens, every single one, and the table is able to hold them. It actually becomes stronger with each burden laid upon it because it knows the strength you will have when you give these burdens over. It is an act of generosity on your part to give these burdens over to the table, so when you are ready you can lay them down, one by one.

The purpose of this table is for you to lay down all your burdens. Start with whatever comes first. Speak or write them down on a sheet of paper. Place them on the table. The table can hold any burden, no matter what it is, and there is nothing too heavy for it. Whatever is weighing on you, give it to the table. There's nothing too big or burdensome for it. It doesn't judge. Tell it anything. It can handle the weight of any burden. Lay it down. No matter what your life looks like right now, take a deep breath, inhale and exhale. Now take another breath. Let it go.

What do you want to say?

What burden are you holding onto that feels too heavy to hold onto any longer?

Tell the burden or burdens to the table. Let them all come out without any judgment on your part. Tell the table anything you want.

(pause)

When you are ready, thank the table for receiving these for you. In turn, the table thanks you for each and every one.

Know that you can return to this table at any time and give it any burdens you hold and are ready to surrender.

Now, replace that burden by holding something within your heart that you love. Imagine placing that person, animal or thing in your heart. Place your hands in prayer at your heart center and be in gratitude for what you love and carry that love with you throughout your day.

UNDERSTANDING GRIEF

"There are no mistakes, no coincidences. All events are blessings given to us to learn from."

~Elizabeth Kubler Ross

When I discovered the work of Elizabeth Kubler-Ross and her identification of the stages of grief, it helped me so much in my own process of healing. The stages of her work are identified as denial, anger, depression, bargaining and acceptance.

Healing works in cycles. It isn't a cut-and-dried assumption that once you work though stage one and go to stage two that you are completely healed of stage one, although sometimes this does happen. More commonly, what happens is like the peeling away of layers. You peel away the first layer and the second layer is waiting there for you. It is a deeper level of understanding from the first layer, or even a different wound. The action is to not fear the layers, but rather allow them to shed off of you, like a snake sheds its skin.

It is possible to become stuck in the stages and not move past them. When we get stuck, we should seek outside help to guide us through the next steps. My understanding of the stages identified by Elizabeth Kubler Ross (1926-2004), in her groundbreaking book, *On Death and Dying*, 1969, are as follows:

Stage 1-Denial: In this first stage of grief, we reject the current reality and tell ourselves this isn't really happening. The reality of the situation is too bleak and impossible to believe, so denial is our only option. Denial helps us to survive the shock of what just happened.

Stage 2-Anger: Anger comes at us with such an intensity that we often want to reject the feeling and lash out. Underlying the emotion of anger is deep hurt.

Stage 3-Bargaining: At the level of bargaining, we negotiate with God, essentially asking for what was taken away to be brought back and we will do anything for it, to no avail.

Stage 4-Depression: Depression is an intense sadness where we often lose our identity, our desire to enjoy life and things we used to enjoy. Depression is a deep internal and external numbness.

Stage 5-Acceptance: As the last stage, we finally reach a point of accepting what we cannot control, that the event that happened is here to stay, and we must learn how to move on, for the alternative of staying stuck in grief is too painful. Acceptance is allowing everything to be as it is, without needing to understand why. Often in acceptance, the qualities of compassion, forgiveness and love present themselves in order to help us move on.

"Acceptance is different than quitting. It means that no matter what, you won't abandon yourself in your time of need."
~Kris Karr

> **Invitation:** *In this moment, can you accept one aspect of your life that you have not been able to accept before? Acceptance doesn't mean doing nothing about it, although that may be the answer in some situations, but rather not needing to do anything about it right now. Just accept that it is here now, whatever it is, no matter how painful. This is the beginning of healing, and from that comes a place of knowing that all is well, perfect, and whole, even if it appears as the complete opposite, such as broken, horrible and painful. Opening into acceptance is an opening into freedom.*

Stacie Ivey

LETTING GO OF THE PAST

"Whatever the present moment contains, accept it as if you had chosen it."

~Eckhart Tolle

When we can completely accept the past and everything that happened in it, we are free. On the other hand, when we get stuck in the past, we lament over the story over and over again. We replay messages about the story in our thoughts. Is it any wonder we feel stuck, frozen and depressed? When a situation doesn't work out the way we want it to or we feel as if we were taken advantage of and we can't let go, we remain in bondage to that person or people we blame for the act. We can never feel free when we are caught here, because it is completely unnatural to remain stuck in the past. What if we could completely let it go in a way that frees us from the burdens we carry?

When we hold onto the past, we don't just affect our lives, we affect everyone and anyone who lives with us or shares our presence with us in any way, even if just for a moment. Carrying the past around with us all of the time is similar to carrying around bags of trash that never get tossed or recycled. Everywhere we go, the garbage comes with us. It's weight and it keeps us heavy and burdened, both in body and spirit. When we can learn to clear those wounds through forgiveness, unconditional love and acceptance, we free ourselves from carrying the burdens of those wounds, which replay over and over in our lives until we are finally ready to face them with confidence and conviction.

> **Invitation:** *Think of something you have been holding onto for a period of time, months, years, or even decades.*
> - *What is it?*
> - *Why are you holding onto it?*

- *Who is it hurting more by holding onto it, you or the person who did the act to you?*
- *What are you gaining by holding onto this hurt?*
- *Is there a part of you that feels justified in holding onto this hurt?*
- *Now think about what it would be like to let it*
- *The past is affecting your present moment because it hasn't been forgiven or healed.*
- *You deserve to no longer carry the burden of this pain.*
- *What do you need to do to release this?*
- *Can you release this now?*

Visualization: *Imagine the issue you are holding onto. It can be from the past or something affecting you that is still continuing today. Both are influencing your present moment happiness. Take the issue and place it into a beautiful box. Wrap the box with beautiful wrapping paper and then tie a beautiful bow around it. Now imagine the box becomes like a helium balloon. Allow it to flow up and away the way a freshly blown helium balloon would. See the image of the beautiful box going up into the sky with your issue in it. Allow God/Goddess to take the box as it floats away. Trust and give it to the Divine. Spirit has it. You can let it go.*

LETTING GO OF JUDGMENT

"The primary cause of unhappiness is never the situation but your thoughts about it."
~Eckhart Tolle

We judge because we have been conditioned into believing in a judgmental God. We were raised believing that God is like Santa Claus, like in the song, Santa Claus is coming to town:

*"He sees you when you're sleeping, He knows when you're
awake. He knows if you've been bad or good, so be good
for goodness sake."*
~James 'Haven' Gillespie and John Frederick Coots (1934)

What!?!? We have been raised to believe in this "story" and whether we realize it or not, we operate out of this story. "If I don't act a certain way, I'm not good and in order for me to be good, you must be bad." It's childish and it comes from the inner child archetype we all have within us. The inner child can take a back seat or a front seat in our reality, depending on our level of emotional and spiritual maturity.

We judge so much in our lives; we often don't even realize how much we are doing it. It's just like thinking. We are thinking so much, unconsciously, we aren't even aware until we begin to become aware through practices like yoga and meditation. When we can create a place for allowing, letting go and letting God, stepping out of polarity, then we experience true freedom.

Invitation: Ask yourself the following questions:
- *What if I could live in a world where I feel free from judgment?*
- *What if I could let go of the idea that no one is judging me?*
- *What if I could let go of all the stories I tell myself?*
- *What if I could allow myself to be completely me without fear of rejection or repercussions?*
- *Who would I be then?*

STEP 2: IDENTIFY THE CAUS
SUFFERING

"Out of suffering have emerged the strongest souls; the most massive characters are seared with scars."

~Kahlil Gabrin

We suffer when we identify with the external, superficial world; the world of conditioning, roles, and ego. Remember the acronym for ego: Edging God Out. When we get caught in judgment and believe the lies that we aren't good enough, smart enough, pretty enough or worthy enough to do, have, or just simply be, it creates separation and suffering. We suffer when we forget we are connected to everyone and everything, when we believe we are separate and not good enough. We suffer when we forget who we truly are, which is eternal, beautiful, whole and complete. When we suffer, we get caught in the illusion of the world and forget we are one with God.

When we believe the world is unsafe and get caught up in the messages of the world, including the news media, marketing, cultural messages, and the childhood messages from our family, we suffer. We suffer when we identify with the illusion that we are finite beings who are here as bodies that eventually age and die. We suffer when we see the world as a grouping of objects and concepts and only see through the five senses.

When we believe "the lie," we suffer. The lie is when we believe the world is the way we see it and think this is the only way it is. If a bumblebee, for example, believes the world is black and white, would it be true? Yes and no. To the bumblebee, it is true because black and white is the experience of the bumblebee. The bumblebee, as far as we know, doesn't have the intelligence we have and yet we believe the world is largely composed of only what we experience through what we see, hear, smell, taste, and touch.

When we see the world through the reality of our five senses and believe this is all there is, we see life from a very limited perspective. This becomes our reality because this is where we focus. Right now, the belief in the limited reality of the five senses is where our world operates most of the time. The world as we know it reflects itself back to us, but we can create the world we want. The world we have now, we have created collectively, but we can create a new world.

We must understand that we believe the world is as we see it. When we forget to see beyond the senses, we then forget to open to other possibilities because we feel comfortable where we are. We want to feel safe and protected. We crave certainty, but in reality, certainty doesn't exist. We resist change, but in reality, change is the only constant we can count on. What we experience in life is what we believe. If we believe something isn't possible, that is what we experience. When we close ourselves off to the magic, we get a world without magic. We experience a flat world of concepts and opinions and a loss of brilliance, creativity and light.

We suffer when we see the world through the lens of concepts and labels. Life becomes a plethora of ideas, which turn our reality flat. We use the labels we have been taught about what each "thing" is called by a name, such as a tree, a squirrel, and a boat, which limits the wonder. We suffer when we identify with the roles we have been given and then, in turn, give others and ourselves, such as the family roles of mother and daughter, the career roles of nurse and accountant, and the ideas that we are the houses we live in and the cars we drive. Connections are good, such as the connections between families. But when we identify with these connections too much and begin to play out roles, that's where the problems start, because that is where expectations about how to behave and relate come in.

Most of all, we suffer when we approach life through the lens of judgment. We judge others for the ways they look and behave. And even deeper than that, we judge ourselves. We compare and compete. We believe we aren't enough and need more to be happy, but the happiness never comes with more, so we want even more, and even if that comes, it's still never enough and we want more. When we are in this place, we are coming from the false sense of identity. In this place, we identify with the world from the place of the ego. The ego isn't bad; it is the part of us that is meant to keep us safe in the world. It identifies with our personality, possessions, and roles.

We begin to suffer when something happens that doesn't fit with the reality we identify with through the ego as primarily who we are, which is our false identity. We suffer when who we believe we are gets taken away. For example, when we believe who we are is a role such as wife, mother, or professional woman, and we identify with that as our primary self, the loss of that marriage, child or career becomes unbearable because suddenly we don't know who we are anymore. This doesn't mean we shouldn't feel grief, however, the intense loss is meant to show us there is more to us than that and also, our attachment is based on our belief system. When we lose a loved one, for example, and we believe that loved one is gone forever, our grief is much more intense than if we believe our loved one is still with us. When we don't believe this is true and get attached to the physical reality alone, we feel lost, powerless, and don't know where to turn.

When we are lost in suffering, there is a tendency to turn to things outside of us that will bring us comfort, like food, alcohol, shopping, drugs, or sex. When we look to external, fleeting pleasures to fill the void, this can lead to addiction. We detach and disengage. We look for a solution to the problem outside of us. We hope there is an end to our suffering and we place a bandage on it for a while. Eventually, that bandage becomes a crutch and later can become the thing that destroys us, or at least that's what we think.

That little thing that becomes bigger the more we ignore it becomes the thing we eventually have to address, whether we like to or not. Some of us may never choose to address it and in that case, life has a way of self-correcting. This self-correction may result in disease, divorce, or even death. Whatever happens, life places us where we no longer have a choice to behave the same way we behaved before.

The knocks in our lives become louder until we listen. The knocks may begin as a tiny tap or a faint whisper, which turns into a touch and a word, then leads to a push or a scream and eventually becomes a full-blown tsunami. Some of us never get the message, but many of us do. We get a big memo that something's not right in the way we are operating and see the world when a big event happens that causes a paradigm shift of who we think we are. Usually, for us to awaken out of the dream of who we think we are and what the world we live in really is, beyond the world of concepts and into the world of magic, there is a catastrophic event that gets us there. That event, whether it is a major loss, such as a divorce, loss of a loved one through death or separation, or a health crisis, can be the wake-up call to awaken us from the dream of illusion that this world, filled with the roles, beliefs, conditioning and concepts is all there is. This kind of event comes at us face to face and causes us to take a deep hard look at whether or not this is true.

We believe we shouldn't have to suffer. There is a lie we are told, somewhere along the line, that if we are good people, we can avoid suffering. Yet for everyone, at one point or another, life provides suffering. Everyone has encountered suffering, and those who pretend they don't suffer, suffer the most. It is an illusion. We all suffer. It is part of the human condition. When we realize this, we can support each other with greater levels of compassion and understanding when we see someone else suffering the way we suffered.

When we don't understand, we suffer. When we believe, it shouldn't be this way! Why me? What did I do to deserve this? We suffer because we get stuck in the past and worry about the future. We suffer because we want it to be different from what it is and feel extremely disempowered because there is nothing we can do. We must learn to surrender in the moment of suffering. Sometimes, surrender comes at the point of such extreme suffering that you just want to give up. That is the suffering that leads to the dark night of the soul.

Conversely, avoidance of or resistance to suffering inevitably leads to more suffering, but there is another way. Suffering gives us the opportunity for tremendous spiritual growth. Difficult times and deep pain can lead to the biggest catalyst for change in our lives. They can also lead to continued, ongoing suffering. The choice is ours.

We can choose to turn the suffering into a force for good, a lesson learned that has in some people led to the greatest service to the planet and humanity, such as seen in the lives of the His Holiness The 14th Dalai Lama, Anne Frank, Helen Adams Keller, Oprah, Nelson Mandela and Martin Luther King.

The purpose of suffering is to bring us back to who we really are, even if it's just a change within ourselves. That change has a ripple effect. When we choose to turn our lives around for good, we lead, even if only by our presence, which is powerful beyond measure.

The purpose of suffering is to see beyond the illusions of the world. All suffering is ultimately for our benefit, even though it doesn't seem like it at first. The cracks in us that are caused by suffering are needed to open us to the light and to allow the light to come from within in ways beyond our wildest dreams. The purpose of suffering is to open you more to your higher self.

There is the suffering that comes in the moment of trauma, leading to shock. It is a huge jolt and wake up call, but at first it is very scary and puts you immediately in the present moment. Another, common type of suffering has to do with our judgments and opinions about what happened in the past, which can go on for a lifetime if we don't bring awareness to it. This type of suffering can, over time, lead to dis-ease in the body, mind and/or spirit, which manifests as physical disease, anxiety, depression, and addictions.

There is a tremendous amount of suffering in the world today. There are abuses of all kinds that we impose on others and ourselves including, poverty, disease, sickness, pain, and starvation. All abuse stems from one source, fear. There have been many times in my life that I have cried out, where I even questioned the existence of God. How could a just and all-loving God allow this to happen? Why does suffering happen? The answer I have come to know within my own experience is that suffering brings us closer to God. If we didn't have suffering, would we know of the existence of God?

These questions about why God would allow suffering and who God is have been around since the beginning of time. They have been argued and debated. We will probably never fully know until we leave this body and see what's on the other side. However, an amazing thing that is happening in our world today is that more and more people are interested in this subject. More and more people are being called to something deeper to life, knowing innately there is more than just the five senses we've been interpreting our world from. There has become a profound interest in the afterlife and heaven, and it's only just beginning.

"It isn't the things that happen to us in our lives that cause us to suffer, it's how we relate to the things that happen to us that cause us to suffer."
~Pema Chodron

Invitation: *Go within. Develop your own inner relationship to God/Goddess, whatever that is to you. How you go about it can stem from your religion, your breath, being in nature, being in love, and an unlimited number of other possible portals. However, the answer is to always go within. That is where God/Goddess is. God/Goddess is as near as your next breath. God/Goddess is in this breath. The answer is within you. The answer is within God/Goddess.*

THE DRAMA ADDICTION

"When you live in complete acceptance of what is, that is the end of all drama in your life."

~Eckhart Tolle

All we have to do to see our addiction to drama is to watch something on television or in a movie. Drama is everywhere, so much so that there is even an entire category of movies for it. Drama is gossip, suffering, anger, jealousy, superficiality, and whatever other descriptions we can come up with. We know drama. Our culture lives drama on a daily basis.

When we create drama, we feel misunderstood. We want to feel alive, so we create drama to be seen, heard and understood. Often, the opposite results from our drama. Instead of getting what we intended, such as being seen, we are often not seen. Instead of being heard, we get in a yelling argument because we aren't being heard and yelling makes sense because wouldn't we be heard if we were louder? Usually not, because like attracts like, so yelling attracts more yelling. Conversely, peace attracts more peace.

Invitation: *Can you choose to release the drama in your life? What is causing you drama? Why? Who do you need to forgive? What do you need to say? What validation are you looking for from others that you can learn to give yourself instead? Where can you take your power back by not expecting others to give you what they may not be able to? How can you give what you need to yourself? Can you open to loving and forgiving yourself more?*

THE MATERIAL WORLD

"We are living in a material world."

~Madonna

Today, we live in an industrial world that is far different than what our ancestors ever experienced. Our world is more material and physical now than it's ever been. Prior to the industrial age, we lived far more connected to the Earth and each other. We knew where our food came from because we picked it, watched it grow or caught the animal that fed us.

It is only since the 1900s that we began to see rapid growth and it has grown exponentially since then. The result of this is that now, most of what we seek is outside of us. We are bombarded with messages to buy this and do that in order to be happy. Temporarily, we are satisfied with the external filling the void, but it's not lasting.

The imbalance in our world today is mostly due to our disconnection from this source that is within all things. The answer to this is not by seeking outside of ourselves, but by going within. When we go within, we enter the abundance that has always been there waiting for us all along. What is within us isn't fleeting. It is a well of abundance and life force that never ends.

Invitation: Look around at the three-dimensional world you experience. Notice what your senses pick up.

- *What do you see, hear, taste, smell and feel?*

Is the world you experience more alive when you observe your senses at a new level of awareness, simply by being aware? Do you notice that in much of your life before this awareness, you weren't experiencing life in all of its fullness? Do you notice now the difference of the abundance you feel?

STEP 3: RELEASING THE OLD STORIES

"Share what happened but hold off on what it means."
~Mark Nepo

We wear them as if they were an invisible cloak. Everywhere we go, we carry them with us. What are they? They are our stories. Our stories are the things that no one can see. They are invisible, but they are always with us. They may include the story of how we didn't have the right childhood, nurturing mother or present father. Or the story of how our heart was broken. Or our victim story of, "How could this happen? Why? What did I do to deserve this?"

"Loving ourselves through the process of owning our own story is the bravest thing we'll ever do."
~Brene Brown

Part of being human is feeling broken. We feel broken when we feel separate from each other, nature and our connection to source and self. This is a critical time to pivot in the other direction, to dive into the realm of the unknown and embrace our fears. We all feel broken at one time or another. At these moments, the best care we can give ourselves is to fully embrace those broken places. This is part of owning our story, our whole story, not just the happy parts, but also the sad, depressing, annoying, angering, and extremely hurtful parts. We must own every part of the journey in order to return to wholeness.

Invitation: Starting in this moment, this breath, let your identification with your story go. If you can't just yet, simply be willing to one day let it go. Accept all, even your resistance. You would not be who you are today without your story. You are stronger than you know.

SURRENDERING THE GOOD GIRL

"If you're being a good girl, working hard, and living up to your obligations, but clean living is just not making you happy-change and do something else. You are in a rut and that's not for you, and you're wasting your time. If you are not having fun, you simply won't have enough energy to shift direction in life. The last thing in the world you will feel like doing when you are not having fun is...having fun. So don't let yourself sink so desperately low."
~Mama Gena

The good girl is the perfect one. She's the part of each of us that's afraid to make waves and wants to please in order to be liked and accepted and will go to great extents to do so. She carries with her the inner child who is afraid of getting in trouble with her parents and wants to please at all costs. The good girl believes that to fit in, she must conform to society's or the group's standards to be accepted. She cannot be herself because she fears rejection and she will do whatever it takes to belong.

This is the case for many girls and women in our culture and around the world today, and it is time for this to end.

Invitation: Consider that it's time for each woman and girl to be who she is. That is a major reason we are here. How can you become more fully who you are, embracing all aspects of yourself with unconditional love?

PERFECTION DOES NOT EXIST

"You are perfection and imperfection's love child."
~Sera Beak

What is perfection? Is it having a body with no cellulite? Is it having a youthful, perfectly structured face? It is having an immaculate home, car, or partner? We seek perfection, yet it doesn't exist. Think of the analogy of chasing the carrot. The carrot is always "out there." We think perfection is "out there," and if we can just grasp it we will be happy, yet it is ungraspable. It is like trying to hold onto water with just your hands. You can try to pick it up, but it escapes you.

True perfection comes from within. It is the essence of who you really are. When you focus on the brilliance within, you awaken yourself in a new way. You can have a direct experience of the Divine. You can just open and allow. It is only through grace that it comes and it will come when you are ready. All you have to do is turn your attention inward and allow. It is there. It has always been there. It never left. Love is all there is.

We want life to be perfect and it isn't perfect. It's actually messy and complicated.

Freedom comes in knowing that perfect isn't perfect. Perfection doesn't exist. The concept of perfection is a manmade idea. When we can embrace our imperfections, we allow ourselves to just live and be without having to be perfect — it's awesome.

This isn't to say we shouldn't desire certain things and take action steps to get them. Striving for what you want in life is good. We all need to become who we are and reach for the stars. We live in an amazing time where everything is possible, now more than ever. Yet somehow we hold ourselves back or compare ourselves to others. One of the reasons we do this is because we are afraid we won't be good enough. We fear that if it isn't perfect, it isn't worth pursuing. Or, we are always striving for more.

Western culture, which has now influenced the collective world, believes perfect is the perfect hair, face, body, clothes, house, car, job, partner, kids, and the list goes on and on. No one can meet these expectations. Even supermodel Cindy Crawford said, "Cindy Crawford doesn't look like Cindy Crawford when she wakes up in the morning." It is all an illusion. Perfection isn't real. Realizing this can create freedom.

This is not to say that striving to be your best self isn't important. The great athletes or musicians become great through the process of working hard and trying each and every day to be better.

> **Invitation:** *Notice where in your life that you expect yourself to be perfect. Journal about your observations and then ask yourself, it this real? Do I have to think this way? Ask yourself, is this belief serving me?*

PATIENCE

"Nature does not hurry, yet everything is accomplished."
~Lao Tzu

When we find ourselves in the mist of uncertainty, we want answers and solutions and we don't want them next month, next week or tomorrow, we want them NOW. It's really not our fault because that's the way of conditioning and marketing in our culture today. The mentality is, "I want it now and I want it my way and if I don't get it, I'm going to stomp my feet and rebel because I'm entitled to what I want and what I deserve." It's the inner child wanting what she/he wants and having a temper tantrum when she/he doesn't get it. As we evolve and grow, we realize the wisdom and maturity that comes from patience.

Patience is the act of allowing something greater than us to take over, to know actions are happening behind the scenes that we may not see. In life, it is difficult to have patience and trust that we are being supported and loved every step of the way. When we recognize this and get out of the way, we open to a greater spaciousness of allowing and trusting.

The old adage, "Patience is a virtue," still holds true today. It is the act of trusting and allowing and surrendering to a timeline that isn't yours.

Invitation: *Imagine a lotus flower. It begins under water in mud. It very slowly and subtly is exposed to light. As the light comes through, the lotus flower opens and reveals itself to the world as it rises from the darkness into the light. Imagine you are the lotus flower and every experience you have requires you to be patient for the unfolding, both of the experience itself and of you within the experience.*

STEP 4: TELLING A NEW STORY

"We don't attach to people or to things; we attach to uninvestigated concepts that we believe to be true in the moment."
~Byron Katie

The willingness to tell a new story requires the release of the old story. We create our lives based on what we were told, what we see, what we hear, and then that becomes what we believe to be true.

Letting go of the story does not mean we are discounting it in any way or saying it never happened, because it is important to acknowledge it and call it what it is. However, as we go through the process of healing, we must eventually transform the story. It is important to allow ourselves to be released from the chains that the story held over us. An example of telling a new story would be instead of carrying the pain of the hurt around that story, turn it into something positive that you can share with others about your experience with the same thing they are going through. We tend to get caught in the belief that no one else has or ever will experience the pain and hurt we have, but the more we share our stories, the more we realize we are all going through pains, hurts and injustices. Transforming the story, however, allows us to become empowered by our experience, rather than being victimized by it.

Invitation:

- *Ask: What is the story I am telling myself about this situation?*
- *Am I willing to tell a new story?*
- *If so, what would my new story be?*

THE LENS OF US

"We don't see things as they are, we see them as we are."
~Anais Nin

We see the world through our own lens and we interpret the world the way we believe it to be. What we believe becomes our reality. What we are exposed to forms and informs the world we live in.

We can learn to open up. When we stretch the world, we see new worlds begin to open to us. We feel comfortable in our small boxes because that is what is familiar. It is when we learn to trust that expansion comes forth in greater and more amazing ways.

The more we learn to recognize her, the Divine Feminine expression of God/Goddess, the more we learn to love ourselves, which comes from a recognition of our own Divinity. We become what we believe. When we believe the world is out to get you then that is the world we create. When we believe the world is competitive, then we create competition all around us.

> **Invitation:** *Ask yourself, what do I believe? Then journal about it without analyzing or judging what you write. From a stream of consciousness, write down everything you think you believe about a certain person or situation. Let it all come out. This is where you can begin to uncover and see the potential truths and lies about what you believe that are influencing your life.*

ALIGNING WITH LIFE

"Life is an opportunity. Benefit from it. Life is beauty. Admire it.
Life is a dream. Realize it. Life is a challenge. Meet it.
Life is a duty. Complete it. Life is a game. Play it.
Life is a promise. Fulfill it. Life is a sorrow. Overcome it.
Life is a song. Sing it. Life is a struggle. Accept it.
Life is a tragedy. Confront it. Life is an adventure. Dare it.
Life is luck. Make it. Life is too precious. Do not destroy it.
Life is life. Fight for it."
~Mother Teresa

When we enter into an alignment with the flow of life, we experience a greater flow, ease and joy that wouldn't otherwise be readily available to us.

If we are in a transition, we are likely to question this more than ever. When life is easy, by no fault of our own we often take life for granted, because we just expect the goodness to continue. When we are challenged with adversity, on the other hand, we are asked to go deeper and see the meanings within the jagged places. Often, that leads us to question life more.

Life is a huge mystery. Many of us wonder, "Why are we here and what is the purpose of all of this?" I believe we are here because we are learning who we truly are, at our essence, which is Spirit, and not the ego we think we are. We are here to live in awareness and embrace life with a sense of mystery, curiosity and wonder. We are here to love, unconditionally and fully. We are here to be of service and make the world a better place. We are here to learn, grow, evolve and lighten up.

Life is a journey, and the journey is what life is all about. However, we are often not in the moment of the journey itself. Our body is, but our mind is somewhere else. Our mind is often somewhere in the past or future, thinking about what happened to us or worrying about what may happen. We are stuck planning, but life is happening all around us and we are missing it. Life is about being here now. It is about being in gratitude for where we are and stepping into the fullness of life. The problem is that what is being modeled to us by our families and culture is just the opposite. The culture tells us, "Focus outwardly, be perfect, and trust authority." It tells us, "Don't listen to yourself, don't trust yourself, and you're not perfect and whole as you are." It tells us, "You need this product and that outfit to be whole." It tells us that to be enough, we have to drive the right car, have the perfect partner, and live in the perfect house in the perfect neighborhood.

Invitation: *Trust the process of life. Trust that everything is unfolding just as it should be. God/Goddess has your back.*

SEEING LIFE AS A JOURNEY, NOT A DESTINATION

"Sometimes in your life you will go on a journey. It will be the longest journey you have ever taken. It is the journey to find yourself."
~Katherine Sharp

Where our journeys truly begin is a mystery. Carolyn Myss, in her book, *Sacred Contracts,* explains that we have contracts prior to entering this life and we make certain agreements to encounter particular people and events to help our souls evolve. From this perspective, it would explain destiny and yet we also have free will and choices along the way. Where choice and destiny meet is sometimes confusing. Ultimately I believe the truth is: there is a tremendous mystery at play and we aren't meant to understand until the time is right. This is where grace comes in. In those moments of unexpected grace, we are given the answer to why things unfolded the way they did, and thus it all becomes clear.

Our journeys involve multiple levels of peeling away layers of the onion, only to uncover a deeper knowing and understanding. They also involve a shedding of skin, like a snake. We shed our skins through a variety of physical, emotional and mental evolutions over a period of time.

For example, we shed the skin of childhood as we evolve into teenagers, and then again into adults. We have been told that in adulthood, that's where it ends, yet that is when it begins on so many levels. Each decade can be a new and exciting adventure. We have the ability in each moment to choose to live our lives a certain way or to put ourselves in a box. We like boxes because we feel safe and comfortable in them. We don't like to step out of those boxes because we don't trust what's on the other side. Yet, when we look at the journeys of great people, those we remember had the courage to step out of those boxes.

We are all on a journey. It is crazy and full of bumps along the way. We can make plans and plans are important, but life is what happens beyond and in between the plans. Life is messy, unexpected and beautiful. It is here to teach us. The purpose of life is for us to be happy, yet many of us aren't happy.

Why aren't we happy? The answer is simple. We are disconnected from our Source. We think happiness comes from the external world. We believe this car, that amount of money, this perfect job and that perfect partner will make us happy. Actually the opposite is true. The purpose of this book is to teach you that your journey is to find the wisdom within you. It is to uncover who you really are, which is already perfect, whole and complete. You are love, unconditional love, and you are loved beyond what you can ever imagine or expect.

We are all on a journey, searching for deeper purpose and meaning in life. We all want to be at peace, to be loved, heard, seen and accepted. Somehow, we've lost our way. We've lost the inner connection to Spirit, where we can hear, see, and know on a deeper level.

Invitation: *The journey to find yourself is the most important journey you will ever take. It is why you are here. It is simpler than you think, but can be difficult. It depends on what you need in each moment. It depends on your level of openness and willingness to look deeper. It is amazing, mysterious, gracious, and all-encompassing. It is well worth the effort. There is glory on the other side. It is the glory of God that begins to shine from within. It is your personal journey. It is intimate and perfect. It is just as it should be. You are here for a reason. Welcome to your amazing, brilliant, unfolding, and magnificent life.*

A FALLING AWAY OF THE STRUCTURES THAT KEEP US SMALL

"Buddha was not a Buddhist. Jesus was not a Christian. Muhammad was not a Muslim. They were teachers who taught love. Love was their religion."

~Anonymous

The reason we have so many people coming from a place of judgment stems from our disconnection from ourselves and the belief that God is a judgmental figure up in the clouds looking down on us and watching our every move, judging whether we are good or bad. Doesn't it sound ridiculous? Yet in a deeply unconscious way, we believe it because that's what we grew up with and have been fed. It's not real.

We strive so strongly for safety and security, but the Divine Mother recognizes that safety and security is not found through the material world. She knows this is important to us and that we are holding onto it, but ultimately she wants the truth to come out and illusions to burn away. She is real and she is calling.

Invitation: *Can you open to hearing her call? Consider going for a walk in nature, speaking a mantra, meditating, practicing yoga, or do anything that helps you quiet your mind. Ask. What is she wanting to tell you? Then, get out your journal and write down the answer(s). Allow her voice to come to you as a stream of consciousness, not edited. Don't try, just allow.*

FEARLESS AUTHENTICITY

"To be yourself in a world that is constantly trying to make you something else is the greatest accomplishment."
~Ralph Waldo Emerson

Authenticity is the unfolding, discovery and rediscovery of who we are at deeper and deeper levels. When we are connected to our authenticity, we are who we truly are, without trying to be what others expect or want from us. Authenticity connects us to our true, unconditional acceptance and love of both others and ourselves. Authenticity allows us to be human and imperfect and recognize our Divinity.

Authenticity means we allow both the light and the dark aspects within each of us to be present. In this way, the grace and mystery of life may reveal itself in order for us to heal and return to the whole and complete beings we are, and have always been. It is about understanding and embracing all that we are. Ultimately, it is about unconditional self-acceptance and love in a way that is beyond what we have ever been taught. It is about reconnecting with our true nature and the Source that connects us to everyone and everything.

Our belief that we are separate is an illusion. It is time to step away from trying to be something we are not. It is time to step away from trying to be everything to everyone else. It is time to step away from trying to fix others and ourselves. It is time to surrender. All is well. It is time to ultimately trust in the Divine and allow ourselves to be who we are meant to be and already are, which is whole.

We grow up and think we are all the things our society and family tell us we are. It starts with our names. We think we are separate when we are given a name and learn we are the only one with that name. Even if we get the same name as one of our parents, primarily with boys, we may relate to the person we are named after, but we still realize not everyone has that name. Names have a purpose. They help us communicate to someone else about us. The problem is that when we take on a name, we attach a conceptual understanding about who we are related to that name and it takes to a more superficial level of living. Whether we realize it or not, a certain part of us can turn ourselves into a concept, just through having name. Through the process of being given a name a birth, we become identified with that name. We believe, I am..."(name)." It is not bad, but it is a connection to a more human and personal sense of our identity. What if you had no name?

Invitation: Ask yourself, who am I? Listen to the answer. The first answer may come from a place of conditioning that you are your name, career, mother, wife, lover, or whatever role you identify with. That is ok because you are all of those things. Now drop down into your body. Feel the connection of your feet to the floor and your body to the chair if you are sitting. Ask yourself this or any question. Lastly, place your hands over your womb and feel connected to the lower part of your body. Ask, then listen. The more you surrender the answer without needing it to come immediately, the more easily the answer comes.

CHAPTER 4

RELATIONSHIPS

"A healthy relationship is built on unwavering trust."
~Beau Mirchoff

Relationships are why we are here. We all want to experience the depths of love, joy, partnership, collaboration, and even sorrow with someone we love. Life is greater when we have others to share our experiences. In the context of relationships, we experience our greatest bliss and also our greatest sorrows, because we are often looking for relationships to fill something within that is not complete. When approached consciously, relationships can become our greatest tool for growth, but when approached unconsciously, relationships can destroy or defeat us, but the choice is ours.

Relationships take many forms. These include:

- Romantic relationships
- Parents
- Children
- Extended family members
- Friends
- Business partners
- Co-workers
- Neighbors

STEP 1: THE COURAGE TO CHOOSE: ENDING DYSFUNCTIONAL RELATIONSHIPS AND PATTERNS

"Loyalty is the highest virtue taught by abusers and used as a control tool."
~Dr. Bill Tollefson

When we find ourselves in a relationship with a toxic person, we sense it, energetically, physically and emotionally. Over time, we feel drained and exhausted by a toxic person's presence and behaviors, but this is often not the case at first. At the beginning of the relationship, the toxic person is charming, charismatic, successful and intelligent. He/she says what we want to hear and almost instantaneously begins to pull us into a relationship with him/her. At first, everything is romantic and everyone appears on their best behavior.

Over time something will arise to sour the relationship in one way or another and the toxic person will begin to blame everyone else for what happened, especially the person or people closest to him/her. He/she will make everything about them and create more toxicity. The toxic person wants attention and we want love, so we will often find ourselves sacrificing our integrity, apologizing and overcompensating in order to get our needs met. What is unhealed in each of us individually, arises collectively in relationships, communities, governments and organizations. Over time, the toxicity increases.

"When someone shows you who they are, believe them the first time."
~Maya Angelou

There are many beliefs that we hold onto that keep us stuck in toxic relationships. They are:

1. **He/she will change.** Waiting for people to change is unrealistic and doesn't serve us. When we believe someone should or will change, it's a loosing battle.
2. **I can't survive without him/her.** This is based in fear and is a lie. When we believe instead that the universe has our back, we are able to trust our ability to not only survive, but thrive from transitioning our focus from the external to the internal.
3. **I won't find someone else as good as him/her.** This is thinking from a place of lack which stems from fear and isn't true.
4. **I don't deserve love.** This is a judgment and based in fear, not love or truth.

We have all had moments in our lives where we have been exposed to toxic people, whether it is in our families, work, friends, or acquaintances. Sometimes we may even see someone at the coffee shop and have a sense that they are toxic. We pick up on the negative energy. Toxic people want what they want, with no remorse for anyone else. They are greedy and selfish and they find a way to always justify their sense of entitlement.

One such type of person that is common in our culture today is the narcissist. Narcissism is a mental disorder in which the individual completely identifies with their ego and cannot see anything else. They don't see the pain they cause. They have built imaginary walls around themselves to protect their overinflated ego from being exposed. Narcissists live from the place of ego and see the world as the enemy. They are masters at manipulation and convincing others of their worthiness. They appear confident, yet are actually arrogant and full of self-hatred. They cover it up with their false sense of self and projection to the world. They have a strong sense of entitlement and only have people in their lives for what they can get from them. It is a very immature and childlike behavioral pattern. They expect everything they can get from people and become angry when they don't get it.

I wasted too many years thinking I could fix and make a narcissistic person in my life happy. I was the giver and the other person was the taker. It worked for a while. He treated me as a child and I allowed it to a point because I believed marriage was for life. Meanwhile, I began to lose my identity in the relationship. That was a dangerous formula because when I finally woke from my figurative sleep, I didn't know who I was. Spiritual teachers would say this is a good thing, because it is an opportunity for true spiritual growth. At the time I only saw struggle. Looking back, I see more clearly now, however, it took many years of healing to realize this. Now I can say that person was my greatest spiritual teacher. He taught me the extremes. He reflected back to me the places where I didn't love enough. He triggered in me the places I needed to heal, primarily my fear of abandonment and not being good enough. These were the manifestations of not knowing myself and not loving myself completely.

Invitation: *If you or someone you know is in a potentially violent situation, get help. The abusers, bullies, haters, and narcissists don't change. Many of them are pathological and they haven't matured. The worst mistake you can make is believing you can change someone or make them happy. This is avoidance and it is dangerous. Instead, choose to take care of yourself. Love yourself enough to know you deserve the best. If you are being hurt, leave. Do not allow yourself to settle for abuse of any kind. Seek out the help you need. There are people waiting for your call.*

LETTING GO OF SEEKING OUTSIDE OF YOU

"Stop looking outside for scraps of pleasure or fulfillment, for validation, security, or love. You have a treasure within that is infinitely greater than anything the world can offer."
~Eckhart Tolle

When we are in relationship with another person, we often want validation that we are worthy of love. This sets us up to be disappointed because it is not someone else's job to validate our worthiness. Relationships that are set up in these ways eventually fail because we expect someone else to give us what isn't fully realized with ourselves yet. We expect the other person to complete us.

> *When I was in my 20s and meeting the father of my children,, the movie "Jerry McGuire" starring Tom Cruise and Rene Zellweger was out. The famous line in the movie said by Tom Cruise's character to Rene Zellweger's character, "You complete me," had myself and many other women at the time hooked. We believed that we weren't whole and complete on our own, and thus needed the approval and validation of another to complete us. We don't believe a movie can impact our lives in this way but all of life is a story and our culture impacts us in far greater ways than we are typically aware of.*
>
> *This is just one personal example of how profound and dysfunctional one movie (or event) can have an impact on our lives.*

What we observe and then believe becomes our programming and therefore directly impacts our lives. When we believe something, this becomes our reality.

Invitation: *Learn to shake it off. I once saw two ducks have a disagreement. Their process was fascinating and had three steps: the fight, the separation, and the shake it off. After fighting, they shook it off in the same way they usually shake off water.*

Try the following physical practice: Stand with feet planted and knees slightly bent. Shake your upper body as if you were shaking off a large amount of mud that needs to come off your body. Jump up and down and shake everything, your head, face, arms, legs and whole body. You can even make a verbal sigh of release. Let it all go and see if you feel lighter and better afterwards.

RETURN TO SENDER

"There is a huge amount of freedom that comes when you take nothing personally."
~Don Miguel Ruiz

What others do has nothing to do with us. We can't take anything personally, even when something is directed at us. Say someone calls someone else a name. Who is that really about? It is only about the person who said it. It is up to the person who the attack was directed at as to whether or not they want to take it on within themselves. Nothing anyone does or says has anything to do with us. They are living their own reality in their own world and it is a different reality and world than the one you live in.

"Always stay in your own movie."
~Ken Kesey

Recognize that people who are haters hate themselves. If they are hurting others, they hurt within themselves. Anything anyone else does is none of your business; unless it causes you or someone else harm, and then you must do something if you can. This is not a problem for you to fix. If they want help, they will seek it. The only thing you can do is what is within your power to do. This may mean removing a person who is toxic from your life. It also may be energetically setting up boundaries when you have to be around them. Sometimes we don't have the luxury of leaving a toxic person, such as a child with a toxic parent or if we have a toxic sibling or a housemate who can't immediately leave.

Many people like this are so disconnected from their inner wounds and hurts that they just react and won't look at themselves. It is easier than changing, which is the path that only the strong can take. The haters are going to hate. They just are. Don't waste your time expecting or hoping they can change. Allow them to be what they are and are not and leave them alone.

Invitation:

- *If you feel someone is trying to hurt, bully, belittle or anger you, return their energy back to them. It is about taking care of you. Energetically, you can close your eyes and push your hands away from you as you breathe out, imagining giving their energy back to them.*

- *Wear a protective stone such as lava, hematite, snowflake obsidian or black onyx. If you believe in the power of crystals, this can help you feel more grounded as well as keep an energetic boundary of protection around you.*

Stacie Ivey

UNDERSTANDING FEAR AND PUNISHMENT

"If you don't know the nature of fear, then you can never be fearless."
~Pema Chodron

The current state of our world is based largely in old belief systems centered around fear, which leads to control and punishment when we step out of line. The deeply rooted belief is that we are separate from everyone and everything, and thus have to protect and cling to what we believe we own because there is only so much to go around. It is a survival mentality built in the belief system of lack. From this mentality, all we see is smallness. From this mentality, all we see is our small selves, who are alone in the world and who don't have enough. From this place, it is very destructive, not only to ourselves, but to those around us. It is hateful, filled with jealousy and anger. Those are the expressions, but underlying those expressions is one thing: fear. Fear stems from the over-identification with the false self, or ego. The ego is the part of us that predicts the future, sabotages, loves to play the victim, is hateful and vengeful and believes it will never have enough, so it goes after what it wants at all costs. Therefore, its tactics are never-ending and it won't back down because it fears losing control. It deeply fears death.

When the ego is in control, there is no room for God or our connection to the vast and unlimited higher Divine self, our true self. The ego's purpose is to keep us safe in the world. The problem is that, when the ego is unbalanced, it creates a sense of separateness that leads to conflict, both internally and externally.

There have been countless times in my life where I was afraid to leap because I was afraid of failure and I didn't believe I deserved abundant success. I was afraid I wouldn't be perfect.

I was living in fear. One day, my spiritual teacher asked me,
"What if fear isn't real? What if FEAR is:
F=false
E=evidence
A=appearing
R=real?"
I never thought of it quite in that way.

Fear grabs us. It holds us and every part of it makes us think
it is real, because it feels real. Fear paralyzes us. It tells us,
you can't do this because that will happen.

When we fear, we are preventing ourselves from living fully. Fear is an inborn component of our primal brain. It is based in the amygdala and is there for the purpose of survival. It is linked to our gut instinct, which tells us to immediately fight, run or freeze. It has been around since the beginning of humanity. The problem is that now, in a time where we are overrun with stimuli, overworked, overburdened and just stressed to the max, the primal brain gets confused. It tells us to react as if we are being attacked by a saber tooth tiger, when in fact, our survival may not actually be in danger. Often, it is about taking a step back and observing the situation from afar, rather than reacting. When we recognize this is a pattern of our brain and step away, we have time to transition from a reactive state to a reflective state.

Invitation: *What do you fear? Fear feels real because your*
body tells you it's real. Fear is meant to keep us safe, but can
also hold us back when the fear is unproductive. Examine
your fears. In the "Course in Miracles," there is only love and
a call for love. Fear is a call for love. When you no longer fear
the fear, you have the power to confront it head on, knowing
that light always overpowers darkness. Think of a candle that
is lit in a dark room. What do you see? The light, which is
always stronger and the core of who you are.

STEP 2: HEALING RELATIONSHIPS

HEART WISDOM

"Your vision will become clear only when you look into your heart. Who looks outside, dreams. Who looks inside, awakens."

~Carl Gustav Jung

The heart holds a wisdom and power for healing and connection beyond the mind. When we close off our heart due to pain, past traumas or held wounds, we believe we are protecting ourselves from being hurt again. In a limited sense, this is true. Placing walls around the heart can work for a while, but over time it weighs on us and affects our lives and relationships.

On the other hand, when we begin to open our heart in a way that feels safe to us, we can gently and gracefully allow more love in. Having clear boundaries around what is not healthy or good for us is one way to do this. With boundaries, we trust our instincts to walk away when we need to and open more when it's time. This allows goodness and love to come in. The more we learn to honor and trust our intuition to walk away from what doesn't feel good or serve our highest interests, the more we can trust our heart to open and greater and greater depths. The heart carries a wisdom that is beyond the mind and it doesn't lie to us. All we have to do is trust the heart's wisdom.

> *Invitation: Consider, when we can drop down from our head and connect to our heart, we can change our entire experience in life from the place of fear to the place of love. The heart is a powerful and Divine connection to our great mother, all of life, and beyond. Imagine going through life leading from your heart and letting your mind come in second. What would that look like for you? Additionally, there are certain yoga poses good for opening your heart, both in hatha*

and restorative yoga. They include many poses but some examples are: fish pose, camel pose, and placing a block and/ or blanket beneath your heart (at the bra strap line) with your arms extended in a "T" while laying on the floor.

RELATIONSHIPS ARE MIRRORS

"If you cannot be at ease with yourself when you are alone, you will seek a relationship to cover up your unease. You can be sure that the unease will then reappear in some other form within the relationship and you will probably hold your partner responsible for it."
~Eckhart Tolle

Relationships are mirrors to the deepest, darkest aspects of ourselves, as well as our light. When we are drawn to someone, it is because there is something in him or her that is familiar to us. We are vibrating on the same frequency as they are and there is something to be learned from them. Some people are in our lives only for a moment and others for a lifetime, and everything in between. It seems so surprising how in one instant we can feel such love for someone and months or years later, hate them to their core. How does this happen?

The dark is there to show us what we aren't willing to look at or acknowledge within ourselves, and the light is there to show us our true essential nature, which is pure light and love. Both exist and both are necessary.

It could be that person is reflecting a pattern we learned in childhood, such as abuse or abandonment. A few questions that can be asked are,

- *Why am I judging this person?*
- *What it is about this person that triggers something within me?*
- *How does it relate to my own self-judgment?*

Where we lack tolerance is where we don't love enough. We must learn to see that the lesson in relationships is to see the reflection back to ourselves. This is also important to recognize with others.

"Love your neighbor as yourself."
~Jesus Christ (Mark 12:31 NIV)

We live in a culture of co-dependence. It teaches us that we are not whole and complete without someone else. We think it is our job to make someone happy, complete, and whole. The problem with approaching relationships where we believe our happiness depends on someone else is a recipe for disaster. It is the setup to teach us how wrong that line of thinking is. We do this with our romantic partners, our children, our parents, and even our friends. It is highly dysfunctional.

This was a difficult concept for me to grasp, especially when it came to my ex. He was so filled with anger and hate and I believed all he wanted was to destroy me. Could I want the same? I struggled for many years to let it all go and when I thought I let it go, I stepped into a place of believing I could trust him. Then I experienced my perception of a new level of betrayal, which angered me more. Maya Angelo famously said, "When a person shows you who they are, believe them the first time." This took me a while and more inner work.

I trusted that he would have my best interest in mind, that if I gave him what he wanted, he would give me what I wanted. I quickly discovered over and over again, it doesn't work this way. The more I gave, the more he took and the more he wanted. It took me a long time to realize that didn't work for me to give and compromise myself. It only hurt me and it wasn't just in relationships. Whether it be delaying pursuing a career I wanted because he wanted something else for me when we were married or thinking if I give him what I think he wants, that would be enough. It never was. I discovered he would always find an angle to pursue more because enough was never enough. It was a domino effect and an abusive pattern which allowed the betrayal to continue and didn't end until I stopped with my avoidance behaviors and putting my head in the sand to face my deepest and darkest fears that I overcame this pattern and finally forgave him and all of the past hurts, once and for all. True forgiveness was my only path to true freedom.

Invitation: *Consider the following reflective questions:*

1. *When someone is directing something negative to you, imagine a mirror reflecting what he or she is doing back to him or her.*

2. *For a day, look around and see everyone you see as you. Imagine that they are not separate. See the soul within them.*

3. *At the end of the day, journal about your experiences.*

THE LENS OF US

"We don't see things as they are, we see them as we are."
~Anais Nin

We become what we believe. This applies to relationships and everything else in our lives. Each of us sees the world through our own lens and we first interpret and then create our inner and outer worlds the way we understand them to be. What we believe internally becomes our reality externally. Relationships and life are reflected back to us based on our conscious and unconscious beliefs. What we are exposed to forms and informs the world we live in.

Within this knowledge, we have a choice. Either we can remain stuck in the old conditioning and patterns that don't serve us, or we can learn to open up. When we stretch the world, we see new worlds begin to open to us. We can choose in every moment what we want and it's important to remember we always have a choice even though it doesn't always look that way at first. This transforms our relationships and our lives.

Often we feel comfortable in our familiar world because it has stability, expectation, and makes us feel safe. This is, however, a false sense of security, because the only thing we can count on is change itself. Change is a natural process in the world. Nothing stays the same. So instead, the stability needs to come from within in order for us to strengthen and be present with whatever arises. This is where faith comes in. It is when we learn to trust that miracles arise.

Invitation: *When considering that we create our world based on what we believe, consider these questions:*
1. *What do you believe about your relationship or your life?*
2. *Are these things true, or are they your interpretation?*
3. *What in your past drew you to this experience now?*
4. *What can you learn about yourself in this situation?*
5. *How can you love yourself more in this situation, no matter what the current appearances are?*

THE PRACTICE OF FORGIVENESS

"The weak can never forgive. Forgiveness is an attribute of the strong."
~Mahatma Gandhi

Forgiveness is about letting go of the chains that hold us bound to the people and experiences that hurt us. It is the unforgivable that needs to be forgiven the most. Forgiveness is about letting ourselves off the hook of needing to keep tabs or pursue revenge and trusting that universal consciousness is in charge. Everything that is not of light in the world is coming from a place of fear. Being in forgiveness opens us to the understanding that people hurt and create hurt from their hurt. Wisdom, however teaches us that we must also be discerning with people and situations, set boundaries and stand up for what we believe is right.

When someone shows you who they are, believe them. After experiencing domestic violence in the form of mental and emotional abuse, in a nine-year marriage, I suddenly understood why battered women stay. It all comes down to personal self-esteem and the belief that you can fix or change the other person.

"When another person makes you suffer, it is because he suffers deeply within himself, and his suffering is spilling over. He does not need punishment; he needs help. That's the message he is sending."
~Thich Nhat Hanh

I drew to myself a romantic partner who was mentally and emotionally abusive as well as someone who would continually abandon me because I hadn't healed those wounds in myself. I focused on someone who I believed I could make happy and "fix." I later realized how arrogant I was to believe it was my job to "fix" someone else. I had to face my own shadows and realize the only job I was required to do was set boundaries, stand up for myself and allow the inner work to happen within me. My only job was me, with a big dose of surrender to Spirit.

Forgiveness is one of the primary reasons we are here. When we forgive, we are set free from our limitations and from the hardened hearts we build up to protect us. Forgiveness opens us up to love.

Forgiveness has been one of the greatest and most difficult lessons of my life. Pain and heartache can be so heavy and strong. It keeps us tied and binds us in a way that we feel justified in. The reason for this is because we mistakenly believe forgiveness means that what was done to us was acceptable. There are many horrible acts that people do to others in life that should never be done; that in a sense are unforgiveable. This is because we don't understand the true nature of forgiveness. I have learned that we are here to learn to love. When we can't forgive, that lack of forgiveness shows us where our capacity for love still needs to open and grow. It shows us where we need to surrender, allow and let go more.

Forgiveness means to "for give." We are here to learn to give and receive love, whole-heartedly and unconditionally. The first step is to love, forgive, and accept ourselves and to stop being so critical of ourselves. It is radical self-acceptance, for all of our decisions and misgivings. It is being ok with what happened in the past and allowing it to be.

I know how hard this can be.

We are trained to be so hard on ourselves. We are taught it is a weakness to be vulnerable. We are taught everything should be perfect and look a certain way. We are taught it's acceptable to have positive feelings but not negative feelings, and when the negative feelings arise, if we don't have an outside source punishing us, we punish ourselves.

Forgiveness takes compassion and empathy. It takes an understanding that the other person is doing what they think is right or justified in. They will gather evidence. They will prove to themselves that their violence is righteous. Protect yourself from people like this and let it go.

"God,
grant me the Serenity to accept the things I cannot change,
the Courage to change the things I can,
and the Wisdom to know the difference."
~Reinhold Niebuhr

The past is over. Some situations lend themselves to an ongoing act of forgiveness, such as in divorce with children when one person continues to fight and not forgive. This feels like a death that never ends. Other situations, like a loved one dying because of the actions of another, can feel like the most unforgivable thing in the world. However, a lack of forgiveness just eats away at you. It is like wanting to poison the other person, and in the end poisoning yourself because of your own inner hatred.

Forgiveness is often the most difficult action to take; yet it's also the most profound release. And, most profound of all, it may take forgiving yourself first. You don't serve the world, let alone yourself, by holding onto beating yourself up over a lack of forgiveness. You can't expect forgiveness from someone else; you can only give it to yourself. Forgiveness helps you grow beyond yourself and into the truth that you are so much more.

> **Invitation:** *Ask yourself, "Who do I need to forgive? Who do I think is the most wrong and unjust person or group? Who is unforgivable?" Whatever comes first is where you start. You can journal about how angry you are and just let it all come out. Don't judge what comes out. Just write it all out. An unlined art journal is best but a legal pad works well too. It doesn't need to be fancy. Normal paper is best. That way you can let it all out and not worry about it being pretty.*

> **Note:** *If you are in an abusive relationship, do what you can to get yourself out of a bad situation. It's about trusting there is a force greater than you and greater than the person you're in a romantic relationship with. The power of God and Goddess is greater than any human. It's about taking the leap and trusting you will be held. It's about letting go and being willing to admit things won't change. It's about taking care of yourself and realizing you deserve it.*

STEP 3: ENTERING THE SACRED RELATIONSHIP

"Learn how to see. Realize that everything connects to everything else. "

~Leonardo da Vinci

Just beneath the physical world of our senses there is a realm more vibrant, creative, expansive, and loving. There is a realm that we are all connected to, yet are just removed from. It is the realm of the sacred and we can apply this understanding to all of our relationships and life. Every living being is sacred and every connection we make is sacred.

In the realm of the sacred, there is no judgment, no polarity, no right and wrong, there just is. Judgment is a large part of how and why relationships fall apart because we forget the sacred wisdom and truth in it all. Egos take over.

The sacred is sacred partially because it is hidden, just beneath a thin layer of veil that is completely accessible, yet blocked. Paradoxically it is right here, right now for all of us to touch and experience at the deepest and most profound levels instantaneously, yet in another way it is the most difficult concept of all to grasp. Why? Because it is not something to grasp or achieve, it already is. When we can grasp this from within, we can apply it to all relationships.

The sacred can be seen and felt through our connection to our body. All the answers and wisdom are within us, at all times. We can find it through our heart and we can find it through our third eye. Our heart is innately filled with an expansive wisdom greater than the mind, and our third eye allows us to see beyond what our physical eyes can see. When the veil that is put in place by our conditions and perceived limitations is lifted, we are free and the world becomes alive in a new way. Blocks are removed, relationships are closer and more connected and our lives can be lived the way they are meant to be lived, with harmony and ease.

LOVING YOU

"There is only love or a call for love."
~A Course in Miracles

The sacred relationship can take many forms, such as romantic partnerships, but also parent-child relationships and even business partners. We often think of relationships involving others, but we forget about the most important relationship. It is the one you have with yourself.

Somewhere in our childhoods we were taught we weren't enough and that we had to be something different from who we were to be loved. The problem is not that we were taught this lie, but that we believed it. When we believe something, we think it to be true and then internalize it. From there, everything we do allows this to play out in one way or another so that it cannot be seen as the lie it is. That is what our spiritual work is, to shine a light on the darkness that is keeping us from the understanding that who we are is not who we think we are, so that we can be free from it. We are meant to shine our light, which just through our presence gives others permission to do the same.

Deep within each of us is the innate desire to be loved. This is because love is our natural state. There is no other state than love. However, when we don't love ourselves, we seek validation of love from others. Conflict can start when we do not get the validation we are looking for. This usually begins a vicious cycle of disconnected human traits in relationships such as name calling, jealousy, belittlement, anger, rage — the list could go on forever. When we don't love ourselves, our relationships mirror that lack of love. The reason this mirror exists is for us to see what we aren't seeing, to turn the mirror around so we can actually look at it, which actually takes the power it has over us away. But because we are so afraid of it, we are afraid to look at it.

When we don't love ourselves, we place walls around ourselves, energetically and often subconsciously because we don't want to get hurt. We justify this because we have been hurt before and we fear our hearts breaking, so we block ourselves from receiving love. Then love becomes the seeking that we never find. It is like the carrot on a string held out in front of us just enough that we see it but we can never grasp it because it is just out of our reach.

Instead, we must know we are love. When we act from a place of knowing we are love, we radiate love outward through our presence that holds the space for love and in turn, love gets radiated back to us. Love is unlimited and abundant. There is no lack of love.

When I gave birth to my firstborn child, my beautiful daughter, she opened me to a level of love I had yet to experience. It was an unlimited and unconditional feeling of love that I had never experienced in the same way with another person. Then, when it was time to give birth to my second child, my son, I thought, how can I love him as much as I love her? Will the love just be equally divided in half? No, it doubled. There are no limits to love. The only limits are the false beliefs about love that our minds hold.

Invitation: Are you willing to allow yourself to open to love yourself more, and then more, and then even more?

BALANCING THE FEMININE AND MASCULINE

"Extremes are easy. Strive for balance."
~Colin Wright

In the Tantric yoga tradition, there is a dance that is between the masculine form of God, or Shiva, and the feminine form of God, or Shakti. They are the Divine forms of both masculine and feminine, married together to make one. The masculine, Shiva, is the creator and impregnates Shakti with Divine consciousness. Shakti is all forms of creation made manifest. In this Divine marriage of balance between the two aspects of the one God, Shiva (Divine Masculine), holds the space for Shakti (Divine Feminine), to play and create. Shiva is the sun and the space that holds all things. Shakti is the receiver and the energy of play, which allows all to be manifested in her fertility to create abundance, growth and life, in the form of plants, animals, humans and also art, business ideas, and anything that comes as inspiration.

As described previously, Chinese symbol of yin/yang is also about this balance of feminine (yin) and masculine (yang) energies. The yin is the dark, receptive energy that goes within and allows. The yang is the light, forceful energy that pushes forth and makes things happen. Both are needed in balance or there is disharmony.

We can see the disharmony in our world today of an overdose of masculine energy. Masculine energy is neither good or bad, it just is. The Divine Masculine is needed as much as the Divine Feminine, but any energy out of balance leads to conflict. The feminine energy has been misunderstood, and as a result, has been disregarded, demonized and repressed. The return to the Divine Feminine is about learning to receive and allow goodness to come, rather than through the old ways of pushing and striving alone. When we know we are innately good and deserve this love, nothing else matters. We step into allowing this love to emanate us and then we become love. When we understand we are never alone and have a direct connection to the Divine available to us at all times, fear dissipates. The feminine is about unconditional love as well as play, creativity, joy and bliss. It is about embracing the darkness and seeing the good and sacred in all things.

Invitation: *Within you are the energies of both the masculine and feminine. The more in balance these are within you for your unique make up, the more you will feel like you.*

103

We are all meant to be who we are and when we can be the confident, whole and beautiful women we are, we are magnetic in all relationships: romantic, business, and family. Living in the Western world of dominant masculine energy, consider the following to increase your feminine energy and bring more balance into your life:

- *Recognize the light within you and stand tall when you go out in public.*
- *Enjoy feeling like a woman.*
- *Notice your innate magnetism.*
- *When you walk, feel your feet on the floor and feel grounded to the Earth. Notice your hips as they sway side to side with each step.*
- *Dress in clothes that make you feel feminine and powerful at the same time. These can be bright, flowy fabrics or a sexy black dress and heels. Wear what you feel good in and stand in your presence.*
- *Keep awareness that your masculine energy is good. What is important to remember is balance.*
- *Feel beautiful and confident.*
- *Surround yourself with people who love you and fill up, rather than deplete you.*
- *Be creative in any way that you resonate with.*
- *Notice your presence and allow yourself to soften and open into your presence in your life. Become aware of the beauty of your soul and let your light shine.*

ROMANTIC RELATIONSHIPS

"Power over others is weakness discussed as strength. True power is within and available to you now."
~Eckhart Tolle

Shakti is the feminine life force energy that is unlimited. She is the one who cannot be tamed and loves to be wild. We have feared the wildness within us because we have been conditioned through many generations to believe that this is dangerous, primal and should therefore be ignored and repressed. This has caused our deep disconnection from our bodies and spirits and the over identification with our minds. It is now time for our deeply rooted Shakti energy to return to us and she is calling out to us.

When we welcome the Shakti back to the sacred inner marriage between masculine and feminine within each of us, it then extends out into relationships with others. How this applies in romantic relationships is that she ultimately lets us soften, relax, and learn to receive at deeper and deeper levels. She opens us to the power that comes from within and asks us, "Are we willing to allow more pleasure in and can we safely enter a portal we once feared but deeply longed for?"

As a woman, tapping into the Shakti energy helps us see that she has a beautiful power. She is the energy within that wants to play and dance through life without boundaries. Being confined is heavy to her and goes against her true nature to be free, as she is unlimited.

The sacred romantic relationship is the moment-by-moment dance between Shiva (masculine energy) and Shakti (feminine energy). We have both within each of us, and the amount we have of each falls along different areas of the spectrum, depending on who we are and what our sexual preference is. In terms of a female-male relationship, it is helpful for the woman to identify with Shakti and learn to allow and receive what the man, or Shiva, wants to give. He gets turned on by his ability to give. This is the gift of finding that balance and learning to receive more. Many women block themselves from receiving and others may go to the other extreme. As with everything, it's about balance.

Invitation: Allow your partner to pleasure you, run you a bath, give you a gift of any kind and open doors for you.

When we enter the Shiva-Shakti relationship, we play in the dance of opposites. The story of Shiva and Shakti comes from the tradition of Anahatha yoga from the Hindu tradition. One day, Shiva asked Shakti, what is love? Shakti replied, "Love is without any conditions, respect and honor without harm. It takes courage and strength to be that loving." Within the Shiva-Shakti relationship is the scintillating power of Divine sexual energy and play within the form of our physical bodies, minds, and emotions. It is a vibrational, powerful and potent gift that when tapped into, is respectful and safe to both; it is pure ecstasy.

Invitation: Where can you allow yourself to open more, receive more, play more and enjoy more? Why are you blocking your pleasure? Who can you feel safe to explore this side of you with? Can you start with you and expand from there? Trust your intuition and your body. They never lie. Discernment is the key.

PARENT-CHILD RELATIONSHIPS

"When you parent, it's crucial you realize you aren't raising a mini-me, but a spirit throbbing with it's own signature."
~Dr. Shefali Tsabary, author of "The Conscious Parent"

Anyone who has children knows the profound impact children have in our lives. We have one life before children and an entirely new life after children. Life no longer becomes about us, but rather we are suddenly in charge of another being and all the joys and challenges that go with it. For me, I learned an entirely new level of unconditional and expansive love that transcends all boundaries when I had my daughter. Then, when I got pregnant with my son, I thought, how could I have this much love for another being? Well, I did. The love I had for both of my children doubled, tripled and quadrupled, and I learned that love is the most abundant thing in the universe, yet it is not a thing. It is so profound and amazing that we understand it in a felt sense. It cannot be fully understood with the mind alone.

Children teach us so much of unconditional love, but as with everything, all sides of light are contrasted with the shadow, and it is our children who are often our greatest teachers and they are mirrors to the best and worst parts of us. They show us who we are in a way that no one else can. We uncover the hidden aspects of ourselves and are challenged in ways we never expected once we have children. Often, we unconsciously fall into the same patterns and ways our parents raised us, even if we try our best not to. Many times we will say things like, "I'll never do that," and yet it happens to be exactly what we do. Or, we may be aware of some of the patterns and feel as if have we have overcome them within ourselves, and then something else reveals another layer in which we need to heal.

We all have an inner child who is unhealed in one way or another. That child becomes our responsibility as we enter into adulthood. Many adults never reach the phase where they learn to parent themselves. They may appear perfect and in control on the outside, but on the inside, it's a completely different, messy story. Learning to parent ourselves starts with recognizing where we are not healed and not reacting to that wound.

Invitation: When a parenting trigger comes up, you have a choice. You can act from the place of of your inner unhealed child or a conscious, reflective place. Which do you choose?

Stacie Ivey

PART 2

Sacred Embodiment

*"The trees are our lungs, the rivers our circulation, the air our breath
and the Earth our body."*
-Deepak Chopra

The Divine isn't in our thoughts, but rather the embodiment of us. We are one with God and Goddess, wanting to experience the Divine through us. We are here to remember our divinity and our Spirit. Life is about the experience of being human through the extremes and vast range of all of our senses, physically, mentally and emotionally. As we travel through the darkness and into the light, we grow. Everything we have been conditioned to believe about who we are, such as the color of our skin, the gender of our bodies, and the roles we play, such as career and family dynamics is not who we are at the core of our being. Our essential core essence is pure and unconditional love.

Embodiment is the process of coming back into your body and feeling life through the experience of your body. It is a key component into the journey back to who you truly are. It is the process of creating a container for healing and it is meant to be enjoyed. When the container is built from the ground up, then continued surrender is easier and expansion happens as a result. The journey into healing is a spiraling upwards, rather than a linear journey. It is ongoing enfoldment that calls for deeper and deeper shedding away of old skin and ongoing openings of the self.

Each opening allows for greater and wider capacities of light to come into the walls, structures and beliefs we have built into our personal selves and then into our communities and systems, which aren't who we truly are. Spiritual growth isn't a defined process of "do this and it's all fixed when you get to certain levels of consciousness." It is a spiraling of energy and removal of the false beliefs and identities in an apparent non-organized fashion. It's beyond the mind's comprehension and requires faith. We are often afraid of spiritual growth because the mind can't fully grasp it, but the body understands. Our bodies have an internal wisdom. We are only beginning to tap into our awareness of how it works and all its intricacies. When we heal our bodies, our minds can heal as well, because we release years and lineages of stuck and outdated energies that no longer serve us.

Stacie Ivey

CHAPTER 5

RETURNING TO OUR BODIES

"Your body is a temple, not a visitor center."
~Anonymous

As women, we have become disconnected from our bodies or parts of our bodies because of traumas and wounds. We may realize this and we may not. When we begin to uncover the wounds, we allow them to be seen and heard. From that point, we can heal. Most of us are living primarily from our upper bodies, from the waist up, and have disconnected to varying degrees from our lower bodies. When we practice grounding into the lower half of our bodies, we can realize our fullest expression of being women. Feeling grounded allows us to feel present, safe, and that we are supposed to be here.

I used to feel as if I was just taking up space and questioned why I was here. I lived much of my life feeling ungrounded and wanting to fly away. Often, as a child, I would dream of flying. I didn't fully feel safe in the world. Once I got in touch with that realization and engaged in practices to heal it, I was no longer burdened with the desire of not wanting to be here and became free to become more fully myself.

Stacie Ivey

THE SOUL EMBODIED: GROUNDING DOWN

"Keep your eyes on the stars and your feet on the ground."
~Theodore Roosevelt

Most of us are stuck in our minds. We are projecting from past to future. We are planning ahead, thinking about our dinner that night or the conversation we had earlier with our partner. Usually we are stuck somewhere in worrying about the future or lamenting about the past. When we can return to our bodies, we can then be present, heal, and open to greater levels of manifestation.

Whether we realize it or not, many of us are not fully in our bodies. Our souls are living often from the head up and we are disconnected from our heart and the rest of our body. We don't feel our feet on the ground and we don't feel our connection to the Earth. Many of us want to be disconnected from our bodies because it doesn't feel safe to be in our bodies.

Somewhere along the way, we learned to disconnect from our bodies, whether it be from abuse, conditioning, and the modeling our mothers gave us unconsciously from their own relationships with their bodies. We often carry what isn't ours within our body and if we have had any sort of trauma or abuse, we learned to disconnect. It is the soul's way of protecting itself, so in that way it is helpful. The problem is when we don't heal the part of us that broke off, and we stay partially or completely out of our bodies. No one teaches this and so we don't understand what we are doing, or even that we are doing it.

When the philosopher Rene Descartes stated, "I think, therefore I am," it changed the course of our focus in modern Western culture, believing logical, analytical and systematic thinking through the mind is the way to solve all of our problems. We have been stuck in thinking and have forgotten about our intuition. The head bubble has served the creation of the masculine way of manifesting, which is from the head down. It has created the buildings, roads, infrastructures, military, systems, rules, and laws we abide by today. Go anywhere and watch people. Do they seem present or in their heads? Are they here in this moment or projecting into a reality different than where their body is by looking at their phone or other device?

Grounding down into your body is one of the most beneficial ways to return to your place of center, joy and thriving in the world. Grounding transitions us from a place of survival to living the way we are meant to, in joy and abundance. We are meant to thrive and be happy.

Invitation: *Feeling grounded in your body can be as simple as noticing your body right now. Where are you? Tune into your body. How does it feel? What parts are calling out and requiring attention at this time?*

RADICAL SELF-CARE

"When you give yourself, you receive more than you give."
~Antoine de Saint-Exupery

Radical self-care is the most important thing we can do for ourselves. In the past, we have been led to believe that taking care of yourself is selfish and practically narcissistic. Women have bought into this belief that their job is to nurture and care only for others. For many women, this is built into our DNA. And ultimately, it's all about balance. What happens, however is that when we neglect our own needs and treat ourselves last, we become depleted.

When we take care of ourselves and live balanced lives, we have the energy we need to accomplish all of our goals. Self-care is about learning the art of self-love, self-compassion, self-forgiveness, self-acceptance and self-understanding all rolled into one. Self-acceptance is a deeper level of self-care. It is the act of accepting everything that has happened in the past exactly for what it is, and practicing forgiveness.

Our ancestors believed in self-care. They not only believed in it, it was essential for their survival. It was ritual for them, as was everything they did. Everything was intentional and had purpose. All life was respected. Today, it benefits us to remember this and do the same as our ancestors.

Additionally, we all deserve to be loved, nurtured and cared for the way a newborn would be properly cared for. Here are some ideas:

1. **Treating yourself as a VIP:** Treat yourself the way you would treat the most important guest you could imagine coming over to visit.
2. **Honoring your body as a sacred vessel:** Recognize your body is a Divine creation meant to be savored in, loved, enjoyed, pleased, treasured, and cared for.
3. **Respecting your inner guidance:** Allowing yourself to say no when you really mean no and yes when you truly want to say yes. This is both releasing yourself from people-pleasing and being open to receive.
4. **Going into nature:** Spend time feeling grounded with your deeply rooted connection to the Earth. Listen to the wisdom of the trees, plant spirits, stone people, and animals.
5. **Fueling your vessel:** Eat foods from every color of the rainbow, whole foods that are close to nature and grown in season locally.
6. **Moving:** Dance, do yoga, walk, swim, bike and exercise in any way that feels good and enlivening to your body.
7. **Partner up:** Get a massage, an energy healing or go have tea with a friend. Do what feels good to you.

8. **Listen:** Rest when your body needs rest, take time to go within, meditate, spend time alone, and listen to what your body is telling you. It never lies.

Invitation: Start with kindness to yourself. Practice radical self-care. Love yourself. Look in the mirror and tell yourself, "I love you." Even if you don't believe it at first, keep doing it. If you can do it for 21 days, you are likely to experience a shift because then it becomes a new habit.

FOOD AS MEDICINE

"Folks, we are like plants. We all lean toward the light."
~Kris Carr

Food is medicine. Our bodies are made up of all the elements of our planet Earth. When we connect more deeply to the simplicity of nature, it is paradoxically complex and dynamic. Think of food through the lens of energy it provides, not just in terms of calories, but even better, in terms of prana, or life-force energy. When we connect to food through prana, a whole new level of awareness opens. So what does all this mean?

Prana is the energy that makes up all of life. In Chinese medicine, it is referred to as Qi. In the yoga tradition, it is prana. It's all the same. The question to ask when choosing food is, "How much prana or life force energy does it have?" The more prana, the closer it is to nature. The less prana (i.e. processed and with artificial ingredients), the farther away it is from nature. Think of prana in terms of levels of connection to Source. The closer the food we eat is to nature, the better it is for us. It's the same for us too, the closer we are to our individual and collective natures, or Source energy, the better off we are.

When thinking about prana in food, ask the following questions:

- *How close is it to nature?* Was it just picked from the tree or pulled from the garden? If so, that apple, grape or carrot will have the most life force energy because it is closest to its Source. This would be "clean" food.

- *How much color does it have?* For example, a food with deep color, that's not artificial, will have more prana than one with less color.

- *How processed is it?* Did it have to go through a freezing or canning process? If so, it will have less prana than food that didn't.

- *Did it come in a package?* If so, it will have less prana because it's been sitting out of the elements of nature for longer.

- *How many real ingredients does it have?* Obviously food with all real "whole" ingredients will be better for you than food with artificial ingredients. Many foods have a mixture.

Assess prana in food in terms of levels. Here are my levels, 1 being the most prana and 10 being the least (this is a basic list to get an idea, not a comprehensive list):

1. Farm fresh: this includes organic fruits, vegetables directly from the garden that you eat immediately or within a day or two, nuts and farm-fresh eggs
2. Organic fruits, vegetables, legumes, nuts and grains sold in a farmer's market
3. Organic fruits and vegetables, legumes, nuts and grains sold in a co-op or health food store
4. Organic fruits and vegetables, legumes, nuts and grains sold in a grocery store
5. Dried fruits and vegetables, organic
6. Non-organic fruits and vegetables
7. Frozen fruits and vegetables
8. Canned fruits, vegetables, and legumes

9. Processed foods with real ingredients
10. Processed foods with artificial ingredients

Plus, there is another big added benefit to eating clean food, rich in prana. If you want to be a channel to hearing your inner voice more clearly, the more clean food you eat, the better off you will be!

How much life force energy does your food provide?

Invitation: *When you eat, allow yourself to enjoy your food. Feel the pleasure of your food with a new sense of gratitude and even awe at the gift of the food you are eating.*

BOUNDARIES

"Boundaries are, in simple terms, the recognition of personal space."
~Asa Don Brown

When we have boundaries, we are basically saying we respect and love ourselves enough to say "no." This act of saying no comes in many forms, such as physical, mental, emotional and psychological. Boundaries are critical, especially the more sensitive we become (see next section on sensitives and empaths).

For much of my life, I had no boundaries. I was like a carpet that just allowed everyone and everything to walk all over me. This was for two primary reasons: I was conditioned to be the "good girl" and didn't love myself enough to say "no."

Try these ways to increase your use of boundaries in life:
- *Say yes only when you really want to do something.*
- *Watch minimal television.*
- *Listen only to what brings you joy, healing or inspiration.*

- *Refrain from exposing yourself to gossip in the media.*
- *Limit your attention to the news in any form, which is mostly rooted in fear.*
- *Take time away from people.*
- *Surround yourself with only positive, supporting and loving people.*
- *Have boundaries around your time and do mostly what you love to do.*
- *Stay away from overstimulating environments, such as casinos.*

FOR SENSITIVES AND EMPATHS

"Being a sensitive empath is a beautiful thing as an artist."
~Alanis Morissette

According to the research of Dr. Elaine Aron, a pioneering research psychologist and author of *The Highly Sensitive Person*, *The Highly Sensitive Child*, and other books and works, sensitives make up 20% of the human population and are also found in insect and animal species. The sensitive members of each species have a heightened awareness of subtitles in the environment and as such, serve an important role in the survival of the species by tuning into intuitive signals, such as danger approaching or weather changes that affected the group.

In the current externally focused world we live in today full of chaos and overstimulation, sensitives feel the need to run for cover. A sensitive person can be overstimulated by lights, sounds, textures, and other external stimuli in an overwhelming and sometimes debilitating way that non-sensitive people often don't understand, simply because they are not having the same experience.

An empath is a person who feels the emotions and energy of people around them and often doesn't understand how to create energetic and physical boundaries from other people or even know if the emotions they are feeling are their own or that of someone else. It can be a challenging way to live in the world.

There is, however, a huge upside to being sensitive and empathic. Sensitive and empathic people tend to be more attuned to others' feelings and therefore make good caregivers, counselors, nurses, parents and partners. Additionally, sensitives and empaths have strong nurturing and caring traits, are naturally intuitive, dislike violence, believe in a world that works for all, and want unity and love more than anything else. Both sensitives and empaths love nature and need time alone.

As a therapist, empath and highly sensitive person myself, I have experienced firsthand the challenges sensitive people face. I didn't realize I was a sensitive person until my late 30's and when I did, I had an epiphany. It was like I finally understood who I was. Later, I discovered I was also empathic and a multi-sensory intuitive. As an empath, I am sensitive to energy and sometimes I can take on someone's mood. I had to learn to discern between what was mine and what was not mine. I began to understand I could make the conscious decision at any point either to take on someone else's stuff, or to say, "It's not mine. I'm going to let it go." I was taught by friends and energy workers to send any negative energy I feel to the light to be transformed into love, rather than back to the person or people I picked it up from. This way it gets transmuted, such as in alchemy. Light and love heal all.

The greatest challenges sensitives face, when understood and nurtured, can become a sensitive's greatest strengths. Self-care is critical as well as having boundaries, honoring intuition, nurturing creative abilities, and developing self-esteem, self-compassion, and unconditional love.

Here are some questions derived from my study of Dr.

Aron's work and the experiences of other sensitives and empaths that helped me understand the trait of sensitivity. The following questions clarified my understanding of my own sensitive nature and experience and that of some close friends and acquaintances.

1. Do you feel easily overwhelmed by the external world, such as by lights, textures, noises, or crowds?
2. Do you struggle with watching violence on television, movies and in the news?
3. Do you notice subtleties such as color, touch, smell and sound more than others?
4. Have you struggled with anxiety and/or depression?
5. Do you struggle with feeling grounded?
6. Do you cry easily?
7. Do you love being in nature?
8. Are you naturally creative?
9. Do you have a strong empathy for other's feelings?
10. Are you or have you been a people pleaser?
11. Do you feel strong emotions?
12. Did you think your parents don't/didn't understand you as a child?
13. Do you strongly dislike feeling caged in a job and crave entrepreneurship?
14. Do you sometimes feel like you just don't fit in?
15. Do you sense things that you can't explain or you think others won't understand?
16. Are you content with spending time alone?
17. Do you sometimes feel like your emotions are controlling you?
18. Do you consider yourself spiritual?
19. Have you ever been told you're too sensitive?
20. Do you feel like you're hiding and surviving but want to be thriving and/or sharing your gifts with the world instead?

If you answered yes to many of these questions, then you are most likely sensitive. If this is you, it is even more critical that you honor your self-care practices, boundaries and nutrition. You have a strength, that when harnessed, opens you to a world full of life, joy, color, vibrancy, and ease. You have a creative and strong internal world that can create the change that's needed in the world. The access you have to the spirit world is easier the more you learn to take care of yourself and tap in. It's a difficult experience to be born sensitive in a world that doesn't value, honor, support, or understand it, but when you know who you are, you have the tools to become unstoppable.

Invitation: *For every woman and man, especially sensitive and empathic women and men, it is critical to find a sacred practice that feels good to you. Your soul will guide you toward what is in alignment with it. Here are some ideas:*

- *Spending time in nature*
- *Drinking plenty of water*
- *Journaling*
- *Having a consistent practice of meditation*
- *Taking a salt bath*
- *Lighting a candle*
- *Using aromatherapy*
- *Using crystals*
- *Having a regular gratitude practice*
- *Learning more about the work of research psychologist and author, Dr. Elaine Aron who studies highly sensitive people. Her website is: www.hsperson.com. She has a free test for discovering high sensitivity in children and adults, based on her extensive research.*

Stacie Ivey

C H A P T E R 6

HEALING

"We do not heal the past by dwelling there. We heal the past by living fully in the present."
~Marianne Williamson

Healing is the process of removing the layers of beliefs, blocks, and conditioning so we can return to the wholeness that we are. When we heal, it is like removing layer after layer of the onion, one at a time, with deep compassionate love, forgiveness and acceptance for all that was. When we heal, we recognize that now is the time to begin again and to start new, for each moment gives us that opportunity.

Each morning when the sun rises, the birds sing their praises for a new day, because they understand renewal within their being. They are connected to nature instinctually as the seasons turn, the leaves fall and then return again. They are joyful for the gift of each day. The more we heal, the more aware and grateful we are for this and every gift that life brings. Even the dark places are there for a reason. Through our courage to enter the darkness, we find the light within.

We are here on this planet and in this body and life to heal so that we may grow spiritually to realize the truth of who we are, which is Divine. This is why healing is so important. Healing can take many forms, and part of our journey is to discover what works for us. These forms can include energy healing, holistic practices, Eastern medicine, Western medicine, psychology, yoga, coaching, volunteering, spiritual practices and even attending a church or community group. The form does not matter for there are many paths and we are each here to find our own.

During a period in my life when I was struggling, my friend's mother, who was also an astrologer, counselor, and the gentlest and kindest woman you could meet, reminded me to trust God. Trust. Just say, "I am Thine, Though art mine," three times.

It was during a crisis point when I couldn't handle the feelings I was feeling and wanted to run from them. They were overpowering. She told me to say that sentence three times, so I did. It was amazing how comforted I felt afterwards. Something lifted. It came as a form of surrender. It appeared as a recognition that a force beyond myself was with me. I just had to say those words. I was amazed at the power those words had.

Invitation: *When you are struggling, just ask for help. Pray. When you simply ask, grace appears. All you have to do is ask and have faith. All you have to do is acknowledge you are being held, supported and guided. All you have to do is pray, in whatever way feels right to you. If it feels right, say, "I am Thine, Though art mine." There is no right or wrong. Surrender to the Divine. The grace that appears is beyond words and explanation and is connected to your heart. Let grace surround you.*

GOING WITHIN

"When you get the inside right, the outside will fall into place."
~Eckhart Tolle

Within each and every one of us is a power greater than we usually are aware of or allow ourselves to open to on a daily basis because we are often so distracted by the outside world. Our bodies have all the wisdom they need, and within each of us is a power greater than our physical bodies. Everything is energy and at the energetic level, all is possible. When we discover we can begin tap into this innate and inborn power, which can be accessed at any moment, we instantaneously touch a wisdom and infinite intelligence that is beyond this world. This is not a science fiction or even new age phenomena. It is real and when we can begin to use our awareness, body, and practices as tools or channels to touch it, life can and will dramatically change. It is a shift in perception from the five-senses world that we live in to the energetic and etheric realms. In essence, all that separates the two is a veil, which is essentially blocked only by thinking.

Beyond our conditioned minds filled with thoughts and belief systems, a portal opens and is available to us which invites us to the place of expansion. The veil between the physical and spiritual worlds is so thin. The only difference between the two is the vibrational frequency. Physical matter vibrates at a lower level and the spiritual vibrates at a higher vibration. In the spiritual realm, all is possible. It is where love, miracles and abundance are held and can be accessed through a deep sense of humility and grace. We don't choose when it happens. We can create opportunities for it to happen, such as meditation, Kundalini yoga, Shamanic journeys, and so on, but those are only tools to help us open the portal to the unseen and unknown realms. It is a magical world, we just need to begin to learn how to start going within, through the vehicle of our body, to access it.

We do not have a body by accident. We are here now on this Earth in this body to live life fully by being here now. Our body is a gift and a channel to the Divine. The human body is the way we experience the soft breeze blowing past our skin, the warmth of a hug, and the scent of the Earth after a rainfall. It is a gift and it is to be honored. Our body is sacred and holy. It is created in the image of God and is meant to be loved unconditionally and treated with respect and care.

When we go within and learn to listen to the wisdom of our bodies, we access a level of conscious that is otherwise unknown to us. When we pay attention, the unknown becomes known. Listening from within allows us to know what our body needs in terms of care, food, water, cleanliness, exercise and boundaries. It tells us when to go near and when to stay away. It is wise, powerful and all-knowing.

Invitation: Honor and love your body. Learn to go within and listen to the wisdom your body has always had built within. Care for it and respect it. When making choices of who to be intimate with, allow only those who deserve to come into contact with it at the deepest and most intimate levels to do so.

KARMA

"How others treat you is their karma. How you react is yours."
~Wayne Dyer

Karma is a reflection of how we live. It is a mirror of how we have treated others and made them feel through our actions in the present, as well as in the past. This can include the near past and also the more distant past. It can also include our own past lives and even those of our ancestors, if you choose to subscribe to these beliefs.

When we live in service to the greater good and act in kindness and love, we generate the same back to us, which in this case would be more kindness and greater love. Conversely, when we live in negative or dark ways, such as through greed and the abuse of power, those actions are also reflected back to us, and the reflection may not be immediate or visible to our level of awareness. These reflections are less about the actual event and more about how we made the other person or people feel, based on our actions or words.

As human beings, we like to view karma through the lens of judgment, which means placing a label on it, such as good or bad. For example, we would tend to label karma as "good" if there is joy, abundance, and peace in a situation or one's life. Conversely, we could view suffering, destructive actions, and negative circumstances as "bad" karma.

When we experience good karma, we are acting within the truth and light of who we are, our Divine or higher selves. However, life is often not always peaceful, balanced and filled with joy. When life sends us hard knocks, there is a greater good, even though it doesn't feel like it at the time. The universe is always conspiring for our greater good and eventually this means revealing the deeper causes beneath the perceived negative situations and circumstances underlying bad karma. Ultimately, "bad" karma is the result of hidden and unconscious wounds that are unhealed. When a wound is unconscious, we are not aware of it and we behave in ways that act out that wound. A wound can be acted out in many unconscious ways, such as through drama, cheating, detachment and disconnection in relationships and addiction to name a few. We behave in these ways because our wounds want to be seen, heard and acknowledged so they can be healed. It is important to know we may not even be carrying our own wounds. They could be the wounds of our mothers, fathers, grandmothers, grandfathers, children and even lovers. They can also be past life wounds. No matter what the origin of the wound, it can be healed.

The wounds of negative karma can be stored in the mind, emotions or body, and always affect the Spirit because they keep us blocked from our true light. When we are able to expose the wounds for what they are and see the truth behind them, we can heal and release them because they can no longer hide.

Healing requires getting to the root cause of the wound. There are many different modalities to heal. Therapists and healers have many ways of doing this, which include energy healing, psychotherapy, soul retrieval, yoga, prayer, and many other modalities. My favorite is the process of healing through Divine light, which takes you out of the darkness and into the light through creating a new story.

There is a false belief held by most of us, which is a part of the "collective unconscious." The collective unconscious is a term to explain when more than half of us hold a belief that is ultimately false, but we believe it to be true. This belief keeps us in the darkness, identified with a false sense of who we are, and out of alignment with the Divine light within all of us. This false belief, or "collective unconscious" pattern related to karma is, "If we don't see it, it doesn't exist." We believe that if we hide something it is hidden forever, but eventually it will be exposed in one way or another. It will come out through actions that you will repeat in your life through different scenarios that others will likely judge as bad (judgment by another), which in turn makes you bad (self-judgment), and ultimately leads you to believe that judgment. The patterns can repeat over and over in different manifestations, different people, different events, but underneath it all is the same root pattern.

As child born into adoption, deep within me was a deep-rooted sense of abandonment. Abandonment is the root of my core life wound, beginning at the time of my birth. For much of my life I didn't identify this as the root cause of my suffering and it needed to be healed. Over the course of my life, I found ways to abandon myself time and time again. I did

*this through keeping a certain distance from my adoptive
parents, abandoning my true career dreams of following the
path of counseling and instead listened to my mother's idea to
go into speech pathology, and then by marrying a man who
would show up and reflect back to me all the ways I didn't
feel worthy through mental and emotional abandonment and
abuse. The story of my life and my deep-rooted wound of
abandonment remained unhealed until I decided it was time.
When my soul couldn't take it anymore, my higher self set up
circumstance after circumstance to shine the light on her
deepest fear and greatest wound. Only by shining the light on
those patterns that remained locked in the subconscious
allowed them to be revealed and then they could be healed.*

What we must do is first identify the pattern and seek healing. Only then can we heal it, from the root. When the root is healed, the tree can come back to its wholeness and life.

We often see the actions of others and say, "Wait till karma comes around!" This stems from a place of revenge, which is based in fear, rather than a place of compassion, which is based in love. This is not to say certain actions should be allowed and that you shouldn't do something about it when someone is being hurt or harmed in some way.

Karma is not about hurting us through punishment. Rather its design is perfect in the sense that it exposes the parts of us that aren't connected to our truth, which is light. We are all connected to the Divine light. We are all one, but for the truth of that to be revealed, we must heal the darkness.

Invitation: *When you allow yourself to heal through
entering the Divine light, you honor everything about your
story. You recognize you are connected to a spiritual team,
which can include Jesus, saints, angels, and guides to help you
heal. Prayer and meditation are essential. Additionally, there
are many people wanting to help (i.e. counselors, friends,
family) as long as you reach out and ask.*

When you can accept what happened and forgive yourself or others, knowing the person or people who hurt you were acting out of fear and ignorance, you let yourself off the hook of holding the burden of the pain and grief. It doesn't mean what happened was right in any way, but rather that you aren't going to allow yourself to continue to play the victim and stay small. Instead, when you can turn the story around, you become empowered and in turn tend to naturally help others in similar situations, even if it's just through holding their hand and being present with them through your increased empathy and compassion for what they are going through. When you are strong, you can influence your friends, families, communities and even the world in more impactful and influential ways for positive change.

ACCEPTING CHANGE THROUGH PRESENCE

"Some changes look negative on the surface, but you will soon realize that space is being created in your life for something new to emerge."
~Eckhart Tolle

Our bodies are an excellent way to access the present moment, because the present moment is where our bodies live, always. When we are resisting change, we are in our thinking minds, up in the head bubble. When we can learn to embody ourselves and come into the lower parts of the body, feeling energy or bringing awareness into the womb down to the toes, it is much easier to be present. Where our awareness goes, prana, or life force energy goes.

When we are in pain, the last thing we want to do is continue to feel the pain, so we run. Our internal fight-or-flight response kicks in and our instinct is to either attack, run or freeze, depending on the situation. This instinct was developed for our survival and is good in situations where our survival is at risk. Now, however, in the crazy busy and stressed world we find ourselves in, we are out of touch with whether or not the trigger is really compromising our survival. Typically, the trigger starts with our thoughts about something. We are attached and we expect it to be different. The way things appear to us seems completely unjust and wrong. We ask ourselves, "Why is this happening to me?" We are caught in judgment, which leads to restriction in the body and disease.

What if we learned to stay present with whatever is? What if we can fully accept the NOW? It's easier said than done and can be easy at one moment and feel absolutely impossible at the next. When we practice staying present, we are in a natural state with our spirits. The nature of spirit is only in the present moment. When our minds constantly loop us in a perpetual state of past and future, guilt and shame, fear abounds and we feel depressed and anxious.

"Stay curious, share the evidence of your story and hold off on making conclusions."
~Mark Nepo

Invitation: *When life is easy, it is easy to allow. When life is difficult, it is difficult to allow. Allowing is just permitting what is to be as it is, whether difficult or easy. It is being steady through the storm, just as the palm tree is in a hurricane. It flows with the hurricane, but stays steadily planted in the ground. Do this with life. Allow the hurricanes in your life to come and go. Trust the lessons that come from them. Ask, "What is it that I need to learn here? Am I playing the victim? Am I sabotaging the situation or myself in any way?" Just ask and be still. You may get an answer right away and you may not. Allowing is acceptance. It is trusting that you may not have all the answers, but that being is enough.*

DEVELOPING FELT SENSE IN THE BODY

"Body awareness not only anchors you in the present moment, it is a doorway out of the prison that is the ego. It also strengthens the immune system and the body's ability to heal itself."
~Eckhart Tolle

The body is a portal into the present moment. It is the vehicle for our soul that places us here on Earth. It is grounded and when we feel ungrounded, we are disconnected from the body. When we practice being in the body, we can feel more present, awakened and alive.

Past traumas cause us to hold onto wounds, physically and/or energetically, because everything is energy, anything physical is also energetic as well.

We can heal through our bodies in the following ways:
- *Reconnecting to the natural cycles of life and in our bodies*
- *Somatic healing*
- *Breathing with focus and intention*
- *Yoga*
- *Meditation*

HEALING EMOTIONAL TRIGGERS THROUGH FEELING

"Numbing the pain for a while will make it worse when you finally feel it."
~J.K. Rowling

In the process of healing, it is essential that we allow ourselves to feel. It is so much easier to numb the pain and emotions of life with food, alcohol, television, or whatever the drug of choice is. Because we don't know how to deal with our emotions, we lash out in other ways. We yell, we scream, we lash out.

If only we knew that it was as easy as just allowing ourselves to feel everything and anything that arises within us. Feeling, easy? For some of us, the act of feeling is the most dangerous and scary place to go because we don't know what the other side will look like, so we stuff it and hope it will go away. The problem is, it never goes away. We fear it and when we don't feel, we are delaying the inevitable and not trusting that there is a flow to life and a Spiritual team that has our back. We don't understand we are protected and are never given what we cannot handle, so we avoid. We don't talk about it. We find alternatives to numb the pain and we believe that somehow that is actually serving us. Well, it isn't and it is never going to.

When I found my birthmother for the first time after my adoption, 27 years later, she told me that my finding her opened up a floodgate of emotions that she had repressed for 27 years. The result was that she cried every day for three years straight. There was even once that she had to go to the hospital during that time because the pain was so intense.

I have learned the most important aspect of healing on my own journey is allowing myself to feel. For me, the catalyst for my healing was my divorce. It was as if one day I awakened from a sleep-induced stupor to see the illusion of the life I thought I was living. I realized it was all superficial, abusive, and borderline dangerous. On the day I made the decision to leave my marriage, I did it more for my children than for me, yet the strength I had felt like it was coming from a source beyond me. I, in the moment, knew the life I was living wasn't going to change and was only going to get worse. The mother bear in me came out with the determination that my daughter wasn't going to grow up believing a man should treat a woman the way her father was treating me, nor did I want my son to grow up to be the man being modeled by his father, so I left. I left and never looked back. That is one decision in my life I never questioned, and I had spent a lifetime questioning every decision I made and not trusting myself up to that point. That opened the floodgate for me. I began to question who I was, cried pools of tears, and started to learn to how to feel.

True power comes when we are able to sustain the pain of whatever happened to us. When we are able to allow it to be felt, completely, only then are we able to release the burden and heaviness of the pain. Only then are we able to heal.

Invitation:
The next time you have an encounter or thought that brings you into a reactive state, learn to become reflective instead. Recognize that the amygdala of your brain is being triggered and it is a fight-or-flight state. Follow these steps, which you can remember as the acronyms from SOS to BE-HERE:
From SOS:
　1. Stop
　2. Observe from another location (step away and go outside, to another room or for a walk)
　3. Shake it off
To BE-HERE:
　1. Breathe
　2. Experience: Feel it in your body. Where is it in your body? Does it have a weight, texture, color or dimension?
　3. Hear what your body is telling you. Listen with deeper awareness.
　4. Exist here and now, in the present moment.
　5. Release: Accept and allow it to be there without judgment
　6. Expand your awareness by asking, "What story am I telling myself about this situation and what can I learn or change within myself?"

WE ARE HERE TO EXPERIENCE THE RANGE OF EMOTIONS

"Our full range of emotions is our palate with which we bring color to our lives."

~Anne Copeland

As a part of the embodiment of our being here in this universe is the range of emotions we are here to feel and experience, and the range of fullness that they present. When we allow ourselves to feel, we experience the range of what it means to be fully human. Often, we want to avoid the negative emotions and only seek out the positive ones. Currently we live in a world that promotes happiness. We all want to be happy, but the problem with the focus being on only happiness, is when something arises that challenges our happiness, we resist it or block it. The more we learn to block what doesn't feel good in the hopes of allowing only what feels good is that our blocking the "bad" also blocks the "good." It is not possible to only feel good. That is not the way the world we live in today was created or designed. Our purpose for being here is to feel fully all of life, the good and the bad and everything in between.

Think of emotions as a rainbow of colors and within each of those colors are more and more colors. Have you ever shopped for paint? Go to the paint store and try to find a color that matches another color. Only then do you truly begin to understand on a very basic level, the absolute diversity and range of each color on the color palette. There are so many more greens, blues, and even greys than you could have ever imagined. This is just a visual representation comparing color to emotion. Just as there are an unlimited number of colors, there are also an unlimited number of emotions.

Invitation: *What are you feeling right now? Feel within your body and consider the feeling you are having this moment as a color and ask yourself, what would the color be? Then, when a stronger emotion comes up, good or bad, do the same thing, try to catch it and first recognize it as an emotion, which is simply energy in motion. Then, allow yourself to feel it fully and completely. This is the process of transformation.*

TRANSITIONING HEALTH CARE

"Nature itself is the best prescription."
~Hippocrates

Our current healthcare system is broken because the dominant focus is money and fear. We have lost our innate connection to the medicine of nature and have therefore become disempowered. We don't fully believe we can take our health into our hands, knowing our bodies have an innate wisdom to heal and are always repairing and renewing back to homeostasis.

Would it be possible for Western and Eastern medicine to meld into a holistic and integrative practice for all?

Modern Western medicine has undergone huge advancements and transformations. Because of modern Western medicine, people are living longer than ever before. But medicine is missing some pieces. An analogy for modern Western medicine's approach to healthcare is to look at the human body and compare it through the lens of a tree. For example, Western medicine tends to focus on treating symptoms, which would correlate with the leaves of the tree. The equivalent of this would be giving medication for a disease, rather than addressing the root cause, which likely has more than one component. Eastern medicine address the root and therefore the entire body through diet, nutrition, balance, the elements, life force energy and so on. Western medicine tends to address the leaves. Overall, we can benefit from the wisdom of the East and the advancements of the West to create a healthcare system that works for all. This is beginning to happen, but much more work is needed to transform what we are currently in.

Why? Because healthy people don't need the same care as sick people. Simply put, healthy people don't make money for a system that is focused on money. We must seek out our own information and reconnect to nature to return self-empowerment and true health.

Louise Hay found through working with people, there appeared to be a correlation with physical disease and a common linked emotional component. The more she studied it, the more accurate her reflections were. In her book, *You Can Heal Your Life,* Louise Hay addresses this by listing the emotional tie to many physical diseases. For example, for the disease of ovarian cancer, the patient likely had a deep internal wound that reflects the ovaries, such as the inability to have her own children or sexual abuse. In order to heal the physical disease, emotional work is as necessary as the physical healing. Emotional work can be done through a variety of modalities, such as counseling, psychology, psychosomatic awareness, yoga, acupuncture, past life regression therapy, or soul retrieval sessions. Western and Eastern medicine can work together to help in healing.

Invitation: When you are going through the process of healing, whether it is mental, emotional or physical, ultimately there is a spiritual root to it all. In life, situations can trigger something from within, causing a reaction. They show up to teach and be cleared. Trust that you are exactly perfect where you are in your healing process. Follow your wisdom.

Stacie Ivey

ARCHETYPES

"All the most powerful ideas in history go back to archetypes."
~Carl Jung

Archetypes are personality characteristics of the deeply hidden subconscious patterns within our personalities, which were first discovered by psychologist Carl Gustav Jung. Often we are unaware that we have these traits unless we begin the inner work of self-discovery. Learning our individual archetypes is one of the many powerful aspects of healing and personal growth. When we understand ourselves better, we experience new levels of empowerment as we walk upon our sacred life journey. They allow for a deeper, more integrated understanding and experience.

THE SHADOW SELVES

"Until we have seen someone's darkness we don't really know who they are. Until we have forgiven someone's darkness, we don't really know what love is."
~Marianne Williamson

Shadow selves are archetypal and the dark side of unconscious wounds. They are the ways we hurt others and ourselves and reflect back to the ways we were hurt at earlier times in our lives. The shadow selves directly relate to the ways in which we deny ourselves love, play small, and create drama because we don't feel we are worthy. They stem from conditioning and are aspects of our personality.

We want to avoid our darkness like the plague and have a tendency to not look at our own shadows due to our inner unworthiness and fear of judgment. That's the easy way out and it is not the way of the warrior. The way of the warrior is to accept our shadows as well as our light. When we resist the shadows, they persist, but when we acknowledge and hold space for them, they can release.

The warrior acknowledges within each of us that we all have an inner murderer or prostitute. This sentence may cause feelings that are uncomfortable, but what is in one, is in all of us, saint and sinner. It's easy to point the finger, but until we have walked in someone else's shoes, we cannot judge. This does not mean darkness is the way but rather, we must choose love always, in whatever form it takes.

Whether we know it or not, we live our lives through stories and as if we were characters in a play, we operate through subconscious archetypal patterns. They fight for attention and want to take over our behavior because they are hidden in our subconscious mind and body and not yet healed. Here are some examples:

- *The Inner Sabotaging Mean Girl*
- *The Inner Victim/Complainer*
- *The Inner Child/Whiner*
- *The Inner Princess*
- *The Inner Prostitute*
- *The Inner Competitor*
- *The Inner Self-Help Seeker*

THE INNER SABOTAGING MEAN GIRL:

As with all shadow selves, the saboteur acts from a place of fear. It is vengeful and hateful. It does everything it can to keep us from stepping into our greatness and having the life of our dreams. The saboteur wants to keep us confined to the little box our lives, because that's where it feels safe. It says our dreams won't work and that we won't be able to make it on our own. Yet, with free will, we have a choice in whether we want to believe the lies it tells, or not.

We all have an inner saboteur. It's the part of us that is about to be given something and do something to sabotage it being given to us and we do it because deep down inside we feel we don't deserve it. We tell ourselves stories that get in the way and bring the saboteur up, such as, "It wasn't going to happen anyway," or "Who am I to deserve something like that?"

When we don't believe in our power or have faith that it all will work out, we sabotage. We don't trust the process of life and feel we must intervene or control the outcome, which interrupts the flow.

When we embrace the parts of us that are "bad" or "dark" as they are revealed, they can be healed. Only through the healing can true transformation occur. On the other side of it all is the light.

Examples: Not believing in yourself; not taking action on an idea or relationship; believing you can't create something for any number of reasons; believing you aren't good enough, pretty enough, strong enough, pretty enough and so on; procrastination; stopping a project or opportunity right before it's manifested

THE INNER VICTIM/COMPLAINER:

Ok, get ready. This next one isn't pretty. Here it is: We like to play the victim. We are addicted to the victim within and thrive on victim consciousness. It is a huge part of our culture, so much so that we often aren't even aware of it. We love playing out all aspects of the victim.

You may be thinking, "Maybe other people like to be victims, but I don't." I used to feel this way until I was willing to truly look at this. We aren't see what we aren't willing to see, but avoidance doesn't make it go away.

Here is why: We have been programmed to be victims by our culture and it's easier to see a negative pattern in others rather than ourselves. So much of our media and advertising tells us we aren't good enough or complete unless we have whatever they are selling. Media often focuses on fear and subconsciously teaches us the world is unsafe, thus making us victims to life. We see negative images and situations much more than positive.

A shadow side of victimhood is being addicted to drama and trauma. Why? It makes us feel more alive. It keeps us stuck in polarity and judgment. It holds us hostage.

Examples: Intentionally creating drama to feel alive; comparison; judgments of self; jealousy; not feeling good enough

THE INNER CHILD/WHINER:

We all have an inner child/whiner. This is the part of us that wants what we want and feels a sense of entitlement to get it. If we don't get what we want, we whine and complain so we can be felt sorry for and gather the evidence of others that we deserve what we think we deserve.

The inner child relates to the aspects of us that are unhealed and underdeveloped from our childhood. It can also relate to a time when we had a traumatic event or events in our childhood and become stuck in that stage of development. (Refer to Chapter 9 for more information on how this manifests energetically and physically through the chakra system.)

Examples: Unwilling to grow up or take responsibility for yourself; running away from something or someone; blaming others; wanting to be taken care of; entitlement; abandonment; being stuck in survival

THE INNER PRINCESS:

The inner princess develops from our childhood as little girls watching the movies about princesses being rescued by their prince charming. This is changing in movies today, such as in Disney's Moana, but has been conditioned into us as women from our mothers, grandmothers and society for many generations. We were taught that we are not complete on our own and the man will complete us, be our everything and give us everything we want and need. This is impossible for one person to fulfill and a recipe for disaster.

We have been shown that men are the providers and women are the caregivers and as the princess archetype evolves, she may take on a caregiving role. This is not true for every woman but it is for many women around the world today. Throughout our evolution and naturally in every culture, women are the primary nurturers of babies and men are the protectors and hunters. It is built into our physiology and biology and it is based in survival. It has been this way for thousands of years. For women, nurturing releases feel good hormones in a woman's body and it is natural for most women to nurture, however because of wounds and stories, this isn't the case for every woman, which leads to unproductive guilt and shame. We think of princesses always being given gifts, lifestyle, and everything they need and more, but at the other end of the spectrum can be over nurturing.

The problem is not in the nurturing of others, but rather the forgetting to nurture ourselves. When we nurture and sacrifice for others and forget about our own needs, it will eventually show up as something that needs to be addressed because we are giving our power to other people, rather than trusting our own internal Divine guidance, strength and that Spirit is guiding and helping us thrive every step of the way. When we falsely hold our belief in happiness, success or abundance in the hands of a man, we automatically discount our own ability to fly.

Examples: Wanting to be rescued; relying on other people or situations over your own abilities; entitlement; giving your power away

THE INNER PROSTITUTE:

When we hear the term, inner prostitute, we may likely have an instantaneous reaction of judgment of a woman who sells her body for money, however the inner prostitute is much more multidimensional than that characteristic alone and it is within everyone, man and woman alike, as discovered by author and medical intuitive, Carolyn Myss. It is the part of us that will sacrifice and sell our spirit, mind or body or life for the payment of job security, money, protection, status, acceptance and so on, which is rooted in fear. Of all the archetypes, this may be the one we want to avoid the most or pretend we don't have. The word prostitute has a disdainful connotation in our culture, but it is misunderstood. What is within one is within the whole. We all have the capability of being a saint or a sinner at all levels of the human experience. If one person has the ability to be a prostitute, we all do. Whether it be staying in a job we hate or a marriage that is no longer good for us, hidden beneath the lies we tell ourselves is the shadow side of inner prostitute. Yet when we face our fears, claim our shadows and take positive actions and steps toward our personal freedom, goals and desires, miraculous shifts often occur in unexpected ways.

*Examples: Staying in a job or relationship you aren't happy in for the
sake of money and survival, believing that is your only option; sugar
babies/sugar daddies; trophy wives*

THE INNER COMPETITOR:

The inner competitor is the part of us that feels we must
compete the way we see men compete with each other. We
feel we must live in the man's world, because that's the world
we were raised and conditioned in. A woman who competes
with other women is insecure within herself. It is only this
way when a woman feels disempowered within herself. She
doesn't know who she is at a deep level and doesn't trust or
feel connected to the universe. This woman, who is within all
of us, is the competitive woman. "Women hate other
women," is a quote of an old girlfriend of mine. In women
who are insecure, this is true. In women who know their
worth and their connection to Source and their higher selves,
this isn't true. When women get caught in the energy of the
extreme masculine, they believe in lack and that they have to
operate as men, which is often not how the men operate.
Women in this situation manipulate, back stab and gossip.
Conversely, a woman lives from a place of balance in her
energy, she opens to unlimited potential and as if by magic,
she receives, manifests and creates with love, collaboration
and inclusion.

*Examples: Back stabbing; manipulating; competing with other women
for a man or a job*

THE INNER SELF-HELP GURU:

The Inner Self-Help Guru is the part of us that believes
we must fix ourselves to be whole and complete, without
realizing we are whole and complete already. There is nothing
to fix. What we are seeking is already here. Enlightenment is
already here in this moment, now. We just have to shift our

perspective. Everything we need, want and are searching for is already embedded within. The answers we seek are simple. It is in the stillness and simplicity.

Examples: Spiritual materialism, belief in a guru to save you; believing you are more spiritual or enlightened than others; seeking and searching outside of you

Invitation: *Reflect on the aspects of your life where you feel unfulfilled, where you feel a sense there is something more for you. Get out your journal and ask yourself: "Where do I sabotage myself at making this happen and how? What personality archetype am I acting from?"*

Write down what comes. Next ask: "Why do I do this?" Try to feel the answer come from within your body. Keep asking the question three times and see what comes up. The more you open to not finding the answer within your thoughts, the deeper you can dive into the subconscious for the answers you seek.

THE HERO'S JOURNEY

"The cave you fear to enter holds the treasure you seek."
~Joseph Campbell

Joseph Campbell's work and book, *"The Hero with a Thousand Faces,"* involved bringing into our awareness the archetypal journey of the hero. In life, we are given opportunities to truly experience growth and transformation to uncover our innermost truth.

"You are the hero of your own story."
~Joseph Campbell

We can see examples of the hero's journey throughout many iconic movies. Some examples include Luke Skywalker in *Star Wars*, Bilbo Baggins in *The Hobbit*, and Neo in *The Matrix*. Joseph Campbell understood the power of myth and how it directly impacts our collective beliefs about life, God, culture, and the universe. When we are called to the hero's journey, we go through a series of stages. They are as follows:

1. Ordinary world — the beginning, where the hero is oblivious of his adventures to come
2. Call to adventure — a call to action, such as a direct threat
3. Refusal of the call — fears that need to be overcome to proceed
4. Meeting the mentor — where the hero receives guidance from a teacher or wise one
5. Crossing the threshold — the beginning of the quest, physical, spiritual and/or emotional
6. Tests, allies, and enemies — obstacles and challenges thrown in the hero's path
7. Approach to the inmost cave — an actual location or inner conflict
8. Ordeal — physical test or deep inner crisis that needs overcoming
9. Reward — transformation
10. The road back — the return home
11. Resurrection — final and most dangerous encounter
12. Return with the elixir — the final stage, ending with celebration, self-realization, or an end to strife

Invitation:
* *Consider your own hero's journey.*
* *How do the 12 stages correlate to events in your own life?*
* *How has it impacted or changed your life for the better?*

Stacie Ivey

CHAPTER 8

THE SPIRITUAL TOOLBOX

"Be here now."
~Ram Dass

When we have tools for healing and transformation easily accessible to us, we are empowered. A spiritual toolbox gives us permission to transform from places of victimhood to creative, joyful and resilient women. The tools listed below are what I have discovered work for me, from personal experience. We are very fortunate to be given many choices and can each individually explore these and other tools. There are many to discover. My favorites are as follows.

YOGA

"Yoga is the journey of the self, through the self, to the self."
~The Bhagavad Gita

Yoga is the yolk. It unites body, mind and spirit as one. We may begin practicing yoga because we want to lose weight, get more flexible, stress less, or get a yoga butt, but whatever the reason we start, it is usually physical or mental. The longer we continue, the more we learn, through experience, the connection between our body and mind. We begin to understand our breath and slowly our awareness expands to unexpected things. It may become easier to meditate, or we want to naturally eat better or our overall lives come into greater balance.

My first yoga class was hot yoga; sweaty, intense, rigid and overall not my thing, except for the fact that over a few short weeks, I was beginning to notice changes in my body and curious about how the yoga studio owner could stare with such intensity into my eyes the way few others, especially strangers, ever had. Over time my practice evolved and one day I found myself taking a community yoga class in Nosara, Costa Rica at the local and world-renowned yoga institute. Surrounded by jungle bliss in an open-air studio at tree level with the monkeys and mangos, I was overwhelmed by the beauty of practicing yoga in a literal paradise.

My community yoga class experience in Nosara was a step toward my eventually ending up back in the same location a month later for my 200-hour yoga teacher training immersion. We were taught philosophy, postures, sequencing, Patanjali's yoga sutras, unconditional self-acceptance, and that we were multi-dimensional beings. We were told to not be surprised if an arm levitated in the middle of the night, still attached to our bodies. This didn't happen to me but many other in- and out-of-body experiences did.

The teacher training was experiential, embodied and life-changing for all of the approximately 50 of us students. A few of us said we felt like we were living in a reality series during our month-long training and we never wanted it to end, wishing it was our job to be there as students of Nosara Yoga Institute.

Yoga stands for unity. It brings us into unity with ourselves as well as into unity with others. The practice of yoga is diverse and expansive. Yoga is poetry in motion and the practice of yoga brings us into a relationship with ourselves. It assists in bringing us into a state of union and balance within ourselves, our surroundings, and our relationships with others. The purpose of yoga is to bring us into our bodies, which are a gift and a channel to the Divine. Yoga takes us out of our minds, or at least helps to quiet the mind to allow us to feel our bodies. It helps still the mind to bring awareness to sensation in the body, which ultimately leads to being the observer. The purpose of yoga is to take what is learned on the mat out into the world.

Yoga is a tool that helped bring me back to myself. It was essential in the healing of my mind, body and spirit. It calmed my anxiety, brought my mind and body into balance, and led me on a spiritual path that is all encompassing and never ending. I have found that yoga has an unexplainable ability to bring me back to presence, again and again. In my own experience, I have found that when I get away from my yoga practice, I suffer more and when I keep with it I suffer less. It seemed strange to me how it all worked at first, but it really did lead me into to better physical health, greater compassion for myself and others and eventually expanded into a greater connection to all.

Yoga is more than just the physical postures, and includes eight limbs from *The Yoga Sutras of Patanjali.* The eight limbs are focused on helping obtain self-realization through direct experience with the Divine and the recognition of the Divine within. Patanjali's eight limbs are:

1 – YAMA

The five yamas are similar to the 10 commandments from Christianity. They focus on integrity and ethical standards with how we live our lives. They include Ahimsa (nonviolence), Satya (truthfulness), Asteya (not stealing), Brahmacharya (self-control), and Aparigraha (nonpossessiveness). Within these, it is important to remember that these are goals to work toward and be aware of. They move us from being stuck in the archetypal inner child into becoming conscious and spiritual adults.

2 – NIYAMA

Niyama is best understood through spiritual practices. The five niyamas are saucha (cleanliness and simplicity within body and thoughts), samtosa (contentment and being in gratitude), tapas (purification through heat), svadhyaya (self-study to discover the Divine within) and isvara pranidhana (surrender to God).

3 – ASANA

Asanas are the physical postures in yoga and they are meant to work the body, mind and spirit to bring them into a union of one. Through asana, we practice holding postures and transitioning from one posture to another. The practice of asana brings us into our bodies and down from the mind into the heart. Some yogis speak of actually cutting off the head (metaphorically speaking) in order to discover the truth of who we are in spirit. There is a term for the junk we carry around that over time gets burned away in yoga. These are samsaras. Asana guides us to the recognition that the body is a sacred temple holding our eternal soul.

4 – PRANAYAMA

Pranayama is the practice of controlling the breath for the purpose of mastery over our thoughts, life extension and enlightenment. There are many ways to practice pranayama and once practiced, the discovery of its power is immeasurable. The breath carries the life force energy (prana or Qi) that keeps us alive and channels through every cell of our being, every living thing, and to levels beyond our understanding.

5 – PRATYAHARA

Pratyahara is about a withdrawing of the self from the outside world and the practice of going within. Going within is about coming into silence, stillness, inner wisdom, higher self and the ability to trust one's own self rather than the messages of the world and our internal conditioning.

Through boundaries, pratyahara is more easily practiced. Having clear and consistent boundaries is key, but ultimately we live in a highly stimulating world that is difficult to escape completely. It's important to do what we can. Some ideas are limiting television and the news, limiting exposure to negative people, and limiting harmful substances in our air, food, and water.

6 – DHARANA

Dharana is the step after pratyahara. With dharana, after we withdraw our senses from the outside world, we are to slowly learn to withdraw from our internal thoughts. What is wrong is not always the event that is happening but rather our projections, worries, beliefs and thoughts about an event that hasn't even happened. Dharana helps us to recognize the patterns of the mind and hit the "stop" button. This is a practice that takes time to build, like a muscle,in order to turn it into a new habit.

7 – DHYANA

Dhyana is meditation. It is the uninterrupted flow of awareness through concentrated focus. Thoughts are no longer present in this stage. Meditation begins with embodiment and leads into expansion beyond the physical body.

8 – SAMADHI

Samadhi is bliss or ecstasy. This is the ultimate desire of each of us to be free from the human condition and be one with the Divine in all forms, totally and completely. This is what we are all striving for and yet it is here now, always. What we seek is always present and available to us, it is just a matter of discovering and realizing the truth. Within each of us, we know the ultimate truth and the journey of this discovery is why we are all here.

> **Invitation:** *Begin to explore the various paths of yoga that speak to your soul. Your soul wants to play in the physical form of your body temple and knows what it wants. Learn to listen at deeper and deeper levels and you will know what path to take. All paths lead to the one path eventually.*

MEDITATION

"Take some time to be silent and repeat the sound of God as an inner mantra. Meditation allows you to make conscious contact with your Source and achieve success in every area. If a problem arises, then go within, get very quiet about it and you will find the answers inside of you."
~Wayne Dyer

Meditation is the progressive training of the mind to return to the Source of the mind, which is the Source of all. Over time, the practice of meditation can lead to a profound and deep connection within, which results in less stress, more harmony in relationships, inner peace, and greater balance in life. It can assist us in our connection and feeling that we are truly Spirit at our core and therefore we are spiritual beings having a human experience. Meditation puts life into perspective from a place of truth and takes out all the noise of the world, conditioning, and our inner thoughts. It is an embodied practice, which often is made easier with the assistance of tools used to quiet the never ending and unruly "monkey" mind. When we are out of the "monkey" mind, we are in the present moment. The "monkey" mind is a term often used in yoga to describe the ways in which our mind jumps around uncontrollably from thought to thought, worry to worry, projection to projection, assumption to assumption, and so on. It jumps from past to future and future to past in the blink of an eye. It is wild and untamed.

Tools to help make meditation easier and tame the "monkey" mind can include:

- *Engaging in and connecting to breath with focused attention, which is pranayama. Breath is an easy access point to present moment awareness and there are many tools and techniques available, such as slowing down the breath, taking deeper breaths, making the exhale longer than the inhale, and alternate nostril breathing to name a few. Look online to articles or videos for more information.*
- *Listening to guided meditations. Guided Yoga Nidra meditations, which take you through the awareness of the body are also great relaxation tools.*
- *Listening to instrumental and relaxing music*
- *Practicing mudra (hand and body postures, such as sitting with hands in prayer position)*
- *Practicing mantra (Sanskrit phrases, such as "Om Sarvatva Namaha.")*
- *Using affirmations (English words or phrases, such as "I am at peace.")*
- *Practicing yoga postures (asana) which is a form of meditation in motion.*

- *Walking meditation. Walking meditations and dance are also forms of meditation in motion. What makes the movement different is from just regular walking or dance is the addition of intention towards and awareness of the present moment. Feel your feet on the ground with each step and notice objects around you. Then notice the space holding the objects.*

- *Practicing non-judgmental awareness by allowing your thoughts come into your awareness without judgment and imagining them float away like clouds in the sky.*

- *Sitting and knowing that all distractions/sounds are an invitation to go deeper*

The practice of meditation is a process and the more consistent we are with our practice, the deeper and more expansive our experience can become. It's important to keep with it and trust the process. As we meditate, we may experience deeper feelings of contentment and connection as well as a deeper and more grounded felt sense within the body. Over time, often unexpectedly, we may have experiences that are potentially very intimate or blissful and others that are expansive. Everyone has different experiences and it's important not to judge and compare.

All that's necessary is the willingness to practice and daily practice is best. Through meditation, we open to presence and begin to step more easily out of suffering. As we engage in the practice of meditation, we separate ourselves from living only through our limited human condition and open to include all parts of ourselves. Through this awareness, we honor and accept our humanness.

Invitation: *Meditation doesn't have to be complicated or serious. Trust that as you practice it will get easier. It is like any habit. Here are some ways to practice:*

- *Breathing*
- *Feeling sensation of any kind on or within the body*
- *Walking*
- *Cooking*
- *Eating*
- *Dancing*
- *Working with your hands*
- *Being in nature*

WRITING AND JOURNALING

"It is impossible to write morning pages for any extended period of time without coming into contact with an unexpected inner power."
~Julia Cameron

Julia Cameron, author of *The Artist's Way*, suggests sitting with pen to paper and just writing what wants to come out and be released. When I first started doing this, I wrote in big letters, words that expressed all my emotions and ended my sentences with big explanation points.

Writing is a release. When we carry around the burden of our story, worries, or fears, those mental blocks replay over and over again in our minds in a looping pattern the same way a hamster would run over the same steps again and again on a toy hamster wheel. It becomes like a treadmill we can't escape and feels like a form of torture.

When we write, with pen and paper, rather than typing, the act of writing gives the energy of the burden somewhere to go. Writing lets it transition from a mental form in the air down to a grounded form on paper. Just the act of writing is cathartic and alchemical, meaning the energy is transmuted and transformed into something better and therefore becomes a form of surrender because we are giving it over

159

and not needing to carry it. It seems too simple to be true, but is shockingly powerful.

Invitation: *Sit with a paper, notebook or journal and a pen. The pen can be any pen, but one that writes freely and effortlessly is preferred. Close your eyes and center yourself for a moment, connecting with your breath and sitting upright in a comfortable position. Feel your body. Ask, "What wants to come through me right now?" Then sit until something comes.*

Write whatever comes to you and don't filter it. Allow it all to come out and don't worry about whatever it is. Let go of judgments. Use as many angry words in huge letters and exclamation points as you desire! There is nothing to fear or judge. Just let it all go. Then, if you feel like it's something you don't want anyone else in your home to read, hide the paper(s) in a safe place or you can even burn them. For now, just place them somewhere that feels safe to you.

PRAYER

"Thank you God for helping me to understand that this problem has already been solved for me."
~Neal Donald Walsh

We are called upon to pray. It is our service to the one Divine God/Goddess to pray for guidance, healing, strength, support and protection. Prayer is powerful and sacred and it is our duty. It is not to be taken lightly and only be used for our selfish needs and desires. The act of prayer is a transcendent experience from the desperate needy little "me" who thinks we can do it alone to the recognition that we are not alone. The light of God is real.

Prayer is a necessity, not an option, especially in difficult times. Without prayer, difficult situations become more unbearable and more impossible to resolve. Therefore, we are asked to pray.

When nothing else seems possible, we must pray to whatever we call God, be it Mother Father God, Divine Light, Holy Spirit, or any other name that connects you to God. Prayer gives us a direct connection to God and all of God's helpers, including the angels, archangels, ascended masters and guides. They are literally waiting on the other side for us to connect. We are not meant to go at it alone in the journey of life.

"Prayer is taking a chance that against all odds and past history, we are loved and chosen."

~Anne Lamott

In my life, there were many times I felt I wasn't supported or was on the brink of disaster. I have found at the times when my life has felt the direst and broken to the point of no return, God/Goddess is closer than ever, holding me and waiting for me patiently to come closer to Him/Her.

During those times, we must not judge by appearances because the appearance of the situation may seem impossible to solve. Instead, we must have faith. Having faith is trusting that we are always supported and the solution is already here. When we pray and connect to God, we are allowing ourselves to step into the opportunity for miracles to appear.

Invitation: When you are in a situation that feels like there is no way out and no possibility of a solution, start first with accepting the situation just as it is and then pray, daily, every minute if you need to. Do whatever you need to do to make prayer a priority and trust that it is powerful. Just trust and know that the will of God will be done for your highest and best and that you are loved unconditionally. Here are some ideas to make speaking prayers easier. There is true power in the spoken word through prayer.

- *Be yourself.*
- *Speak your truth.*
- *Connect to Mother/Father God as if you are talking to your parent who loves you unconditionally and without judgment.*
- *Ask for help.*
- *Know you are worthy.*
- *Trust that you have a true connection to the Divine.*
- *Read books with prayer for guidance. My favorite book for prayer is "Illuminata," by Marianne Williamson. She has prayers for most everything in the book and a great morning prayer.*
- *Let prayer transform you.*
- *Believe you are being heard.*

GRATITUDE

"Gratitude opens the door to...the power, the wisdom, the creativity of the universe."
~Deepak Chopra

Gratitude is a vibration. It is an essence that when tapped into, brings more to the one who is thankful. When we are thankful for what we already have, more good comes to us. That is the natural law of the universe.

When we hear the term, "raise your vibration," what that means is to think and be in a higher vibrational state. Gratitude is a high vibrational state, as is love, joy, and bliss.

In my own life, I have discovered a direct connection to how much gratitude I have in my life and how happy I am. When I am focused on lack, fear, worry, and shame, I experience a heavy feeling. Conversely, when I am focused on gratitude, I feel light, peaceful and more joyful.

Invitation:
- *Practice writing three things you are grateful for and why daily.*
- *Feel the energy of being in gratitude.*
- *Connect the feeling of being in gratitude to your heart.*
- *Write affirmations and place them around your home to help you be more grateful.*
- *For additional support, I love this author and her book:* The Gratitude Connection, *by Amy Collette*

MINDFULNESS

"Mindfulness means paying attention in a particular way, on purpose, in the present moment non-judgmentally."
~Jon Kabat-Zinn

Mindfulness is attending to the present moment through a focused awareness. The body is an entry point into mindfulness because it lives in the present moment. The five senses are easy doorways into mindfulness. When we connect to the present moment through our sensory system it is free and accessible to us at any time. Mindfulness teaches us to pay attention to what is going on here and now, instead of through thinking. Our thoughts, analysis, or judgments about our experience in the world blocks us from the experience because it turns it into a concept and makes the experience flat. Mindfulness is simple and some ideas to practice mindfulness through the senses are:

Seeing:

- Go into nature and pay attention to the ways the light touches the grass, trees, or rocks.
- Notice an object and then notice the space that holds that object.
- Light a candle and watch the way the flame of the candle moves.

Hearing:

- Go into nature and listen to the sounds around you.
- Find a quiet place to listen and notice what you notice. Listen to the space in-between sounds. Can you hear the silence?

Felt Sensation:

- Breath is a great way to tap into felt sensation. Place your hand on your belly and breath into that space. Can you feel your belly rise with each inhalation and fall with each exhalation?
- Touch your hand with your other hand, lightly and slowly. Imagine you are giving yourself permission to feel love through your own touch.

Movement:

- Choose any form of dance that you would enjoy. Try ecstatic or free-form dance and just dance around. Allow your body to connect to the music and let the music move you, rather than you trying to move to the music. This has the potential to create pulsating and vibratory sensations within your body.
- Practice yoga by attending a class and imagine you are moving mindfully.
- Go for a walk and practice noticing your feet as they take each step. How do your knees bend when they move? What do your arms do? What do you sense or feel around you? What else can you notice?

Taste:

- Find something you enjoy, like a strawberry or a chocolate chip. Place it on your lips and then gently guide it into your mouth. How does it feel? What does it taste like? What pleasure can you receive from the taste of that food?
- Practice mindful eating by slowing down when you eat. Really allow yourself to luxuriate in the pleasures of eating. The more you slow down, the more you will notice you enjoy your food and will tend to not need to eat as much to get the same enjoyment out of your food.

Mindfulness is a form of meditation, where we become the observer of our experience with nonjudgmental awareness. When we can become aware of the sensations of and movements within our bodies, whether it be fingers tapping on a keyboard, footsteps as they touch the ground, the bend in a knee or the blink of an eye, we are carried from the conditioned mind stuck in thought into the present moment, which is all there ever is.

From a higher-level perspective and what has been proven in quantum physics is that our bodies are always moving. When we are sitting still, we believe we are still, but we are still breathing. And at an energetic level, nothing is still. It is simply our perception that the energy is still, but rather all that has happened is that the energy is moving at a slower speed than if we are running.

> **Invitation:** *Become aware of your body movement in this moment. Recognize the subtle movements your body makes in each moment. Open to the curious wonder of it all and allow it to take you to a new level of awareness through simplicity to the present moment.*

SMILING AND LAUGHTER

"Let us always meet each other with smile, for the smile is the beginning of love."
~Mother Teresa

When we smile, it tells our brain we are happy, whether we believe it or not. It is a technique to trick the brain. Additionally, when we go through life with a smile on our face, it connects us to the vibration of gratitude, which draws goodness to us naturally.

Along the same lines, laughter is a powerful tool to reconnect us to our joy. It simply makes us feel good and boosts our immune system.

Invitation: *Remember to smile and laugh often. It's good for our soul and overall health.*

THE PRACTICE OF RITUALS

"Ritual is the passageway of the soul into the infinite."
~Algernon Blackwood

We all have and practice rituals, whether we are aware of them or not. The way we make our morning coffee, get ready to go out for the evening or prepare a special meal for family or friends are all rituals.

At deeper levels, rituals are sacred and help us remember and reconnect to the Divine Spirit within each of us. Rituals are based in spiritual practice, but can ultimately be anything done in a prescribed order. At a certain level, all of life is sacred and all movements, interactions, practices and everything we say and do is a sacred practice.

Here are some ideas with which you can create your own ritual to start your day:

- *First drink of the day: a small glass of lukewarm water with a couple drops of lemon juice*
- *A meditative practice of preparing and drinking your morning warm drink of lemon water, coffee, tea, or chai*
- *A sitting meditation where you focus on breath and/or incorporate mudra (sitting or hand posture) or mantra (a repetitive word or phrase with an intention to invoke something desired and bring a focus to the mind so it can rest)*
- *Reading something inspirational, healing or joyful.*
- *Writing in a journal and just letting whatever wants to come out transfer through your hand to your pen and onto the page.*

PRESENT MOMENT AWARENESS

"Yesterday is history, tomorrow is a mystery and today is a gift, that's why it's called the present."

~Eleanor Roosevelt

We hear so much about being in the present moment. We are told this moment is the only moment there ever is, the moment of now. We are told this moment is a gift, a present. That's why it's called present, yet we are always struggling to get there. Why? Because we are distracted. The world is overwhelming and we are more disconnected than ever. Technology connects us and disconnects us at the same time. We aren't present in the life that is right in front of us and we are focusing on everyone else's lives on Facebook, Twitter, Snapchat and Instagram.

How often do we find ourselves in the company of loved ones and instead of being present with them, we are distracted by everyone else's lives, games and the news and not paying attention to our most important relationships?

Our minds tell us there is something more important to think about. This leads to a constant comparison and in turn, continuous suffering. When we aren't present, we lament over the past or project into the future and this makes us feel alive, but it is a false sense of aliveness. Also, we subconsciously believe we must keep focused on what we are thinking about or our world will fall apart. We must make decision after decision to keep everything together and we must be thinking all the time.

The opposite is actually true. I recommend taking notes in your smartphone that you can later refer to or having a small notebook and a pen nearby you at all times. That way if you have something you must remember you can write it down and then your thinking mind is satisfied so you can more easily focus on the present.

Being in the present moment is about being here and now. It is stepping out of thinking and being aware of your breath, body and surroundings in all the forms your surroundings take. It is about noticing the world around you in a new way and being present with it. It is about experiencing life on a deeper level.

Invitation: *Open your awareness in a new way. Feel this awareness in your body. Connect with your breath. Experience it in an expanded, spacious way. When you can do this, and catch your thoughts as they come in, returning to the spacious awareness, you are present. Even if it's just for a moment, it is a practice. It is a muscle that needs to be developed on a daily basis. The more you practice, the easier it gets.*

Mindfulness is being present through awareness. The easiest way to access presence is through the body, through taste, touch, sight, smell, and sound. For example, seeing mindfully is really seeing the clouds, the leaves, the paper, the pen, or the person we are with. It is about doing each thing with a pin-pointed focus, where we are simply noticing and not thinking.

We can practice present moment awareness through:
- *Unplugging from electronics*
- *Being in nature*
- *Connecting to our breath and five senses*
- *Feeling sensation through our bodies*
- *Meditation*

Being present is about connecting to the world through our five senses and noticing not only the objects, but also noticing the aliveness of everything. This includes noticing the aliveness in both living and non-living objects, because everything is vibrating and in our awareness in one way or another whether we are conscious of it or not.

We can become more easily present with a simple practice. Initially this practice will seem too simple to be valuable and the mind will want to dismiss it immediately because of its apparent infantile and unsophisticated nature. The key is to experience it rather than thinking about or analyzing it.

Invitation:

- *Choose one thing to focus your attention and awareness on, living or non-living. For this example, we will choose a hand, but you can substitute anything else here.*
- *Place your hand in front of you. Notice your hand. Examine it. Notice all the smooth areas, bumpy areas, lines, indentions, and colorations. Notice your fingers and nails. Stay with this for a few moments.*
- *Once you feel confident that your hand is strongly centered in your awareness, notice the space around your hand. What is the space that is holding your hand?*
- *Now bring your awareness back to your hand and then out to the space holding your hand.*

- *Go back and forth a few times.*
- *Next, open your awareness to the space within and around your hand.*
- *Allow your focused attention to expand your awareness further out beyond but still including your hand.*
- *Continue expanding your awareness out away from your hand, then back to your hand.*
- *Play with it and notice what you notice.*

SIMPLICITY

"If you have nothing, then you have everything, because you have the freedom to do anything without the fear of losing something."
~Jarod Kintz

What happens when we hold on to things we don't need? The things we hold on to and "own," end up owning us. When we do this, we are sending a message to the universe that blocks us from receiving because we are putting out the energy of lack. The energy of lack comes from the belief that we don't have enough. In turn, the extra weight we carry because we don't trust that more is coming may turn into hoarding. This ends up weighing us down, physically, mentally, emotionally and spiritually.

Invitation:
- *What if you released needing to or wanting to own anything? How free would you feel?*
- *What if you accepted gifts and opened to receiving, coming from a place of abundance rather than from a desperate or needy place?*
- *Try letting go of what you don't need any more and in turn, see if you feel lighter in all of your bodies, physical, mental, emotional and spiritual.*

- *Approach life from a place of simplicity.*
- *Let go of what you don't need, whether it is extra weight, and old belief, or too much stuff.*
- *Clean, cleanse and clear the space within and around you.*

CREATING A SACRED SPACE

"Your sacred space is where you can find yourself over and over again."
-Joseph Campbell

A sacred space is a place for you to go where you can reconnect with your soul. When you create a positive intention around a space, even just starting with the intention of creating a space that is sacred, the vibration of the space automatically rises and then increases over time the more frequently you visit the space with that intention.

A sacred space has many possibilities. Listening to your guidance from within is key. We are all born creators, and to create a space that is special to you is a practice of honoring the wisdom of your soul. When you listen from within, you are guided. Think of yourself as a spiritual interior designer. Simplicity is important when creating a sacred space.

Invitation: Here are the steps to help you create a sacred space of your own.
   1. **Clean the space.** *Give it a thorough cleaning. Wash everything down, dust, vacuum, and remove anything that doesn't serve the space. It's amazing how good just this first step feels because when your space is clean, you feel lighter and less burdened by things.*
   2. **Cleanse or smudge the space.** *Using sage is the best for this purpose. Sage can be found online or in*

a metaphysical bookstore and comes as a light green bundle of leaves tied with a string. The purpose of sage is to lift the energies that are stuck, heavy, or dense, and create a clear, expanded, open palette to work with. To smudge a room, light the tip of the sage stick, let the flame burn for a few seconds and blow it out. The sage stick should emit a light smoke. Walk around the room with it, setting the intention to clear the space and guiding the sage over, above and around the different objects in the room. When all areas have been cleansed, take sage and tap it on some dirt or a rock outside to stop the smoking process. Store the sage in a jar or bowl, as it can still smolder after lighting. The next day you can relight it. If it doesn't light well, you can cut the tip of the sage stick that was burned to reveal new, unburned parts of the dried leaves.

3. **Create an altar.** *An altar can be as small as a trinket box or as large as an entire room, house, or even bigger. I personally use an antique television stand. The idea is to find something you can use as a base or foundation. You can even use a corner of a room and the floor can be the base or foundation. Next, lay something beautiful on it as the first layer, such as a piece of linen. This is the backdrop. I use a shawl or a beautiful handmade tablecloth that has a vibrant color, interesting beads, or shimmer to it.*

4. **Decorate the altar with meaningful things that have an intimacy and spiritual meaning to you.** *Examples could include crystals or stones, such as an amethyst or favorite rock, fresh flower, or a figurine of a Goddess, angel or animal. The key here is to listen to the wisdom of what your inner voice is telling you. Don't think about it too much; just listen, because the soul doesn't speak through overthinking and analysis. It is much subtler and guides you when you listen. Pay attention to what*

you like. Simplicity is key. You can even start with just a simple candle and that would be enough.

5. **Practice spending quality time with yourself in your space.** *Visit your space daily and keep it sacred. Practice daily meditation in your space and allow it to be a constant reminder of your soul. You can journal, do art, yoga, or whatever feeds your soul in your space.*

6. **Consider applying the principles of the ancient Chinese practice of Feng Shui to your sacred space, which translates directly in English to "wind-water."** *As one of the Five Arts in Chinese Metaphysics, Feng Shui bridges through architecture and interior design, the life force energy known as Qi, which is within all living and nonliving things and therefore connects humanity, the universe and Earth together as one.*

MUSIC AND SOUND THERAPY

"Music is therapy. Music moves people. It connects people in ways that no other medium can. It pulls heart strings. It acts as medicine."
~Macklemore

Music is transcendent, a powerful antidote to whatever is ailing us, and can shift our energy from the negative to the positive. Through music, we can easily access the pulsating and vibratory aliveness of life. Some examples of how to use different types of music for different purposes are as follows (some of my personal favorites):

- **Joy:** Any music that makes you dance
- **Healing:** Shaina Noll, *How Could Anyone*
- **Inner Peace:** Snatam Kaur, *Ra Ma Da Sa* or Deva Premal, *Moola Mantra*

- **Inspiration:** Josh Groban, *You Raise Me Up*
- **Introspection:** Addison Road, *What Do I Know of Holy?*
- **Connecting to the angelic realm:** Jackie Evancho or Enya, *O Come, O Come Emmanuel*
- **Meditation:** Nature, Brain Wave (i.e. Alpha, Beta, Delta, Theta, Gamma), or Native American flute music
- **Tapping the subconscious or dream state:** Drumming or rattling sounds
- **Sleep:** Delta or Theta Wave music
- **Strengthening Intuitive Connections:** Binaural beats
- **Support when suffering:** Josh Groban, *You are Loved (Don't Give Up)* or *Compass* by Lady Antebellum
- **Transcendence:** Sound bowl therapy
- **Yoga:** Donna De Lory, Deva Premal or Krishna Das

Invitation: *Music speaks to your soul. Allow your soul to guide you. Music is an easy portal into the realm of the sacred.*

DANCE

"Dance enables you to find yourself and lose yourself at the same time."

~Anonymous

Life is a dance and we are all engaging in the dance of life in one way or another. Ultimately, especially for women, dance is powerful and transformative because it reconnects us to our bodies and the Earth. It is primal, instinctual, ancestral and joyful.

> **Invitation:** *Dance like no one is watching. When you dance, you allow yourself to let go. As you dance, allow yourself to feel everything that arises just as it is.*
>
> - *Turn on music and dance in a free-form and unstructured way. If you feel comfortable, this type of dancing can lead to a semi or full trance state, which can transcend your dancing into a direct experience with the Divine.*
>
> - *Go to a club or join a dance class that you like. It can be structured (i.e. belly dancing, modern, Flamenco, Jazz, Latin, Ballroom) or unstructured (i.e. ecstatic or trance dance).*
>
> - *Barefoot dancing: Dance at a park, outdoor concert or your own back yard. If others are around, notice if anything comes up for you around fear of being judged. Ask yourself, "What story am I telling myself about this?" Let it all go. Ultimately, you are a free and Divine expression of the Goddess, so stop caring what others think. Their thoughts are only their own internal judgments about themselves anyway.*

EMBODIED CREATIVITY

"Imaginations should be allowed a certain amount of time to browse around."

~Thomas Merton

All artists, whether they know it or not, are tapping directly into the Divine or source energy to create. Creation is our natural state and we are all artists in our own way. We are all natural co-creators with the Divine, but many of us have disconnected from this because creativity is treated like an accessory in our culture. We are stuck on a hamster wheel, focused around more stuff to make us feel better, but when we begin to recognize that and learn to step outside that trap, we become free.

Embodied creativity is the act of creating through the channel of our bodies and feeling fully present in our beautiful bodies. When we begin to ground down into our bodies, there is an inner wisdom that ignites our imagination and brings forth a desire to create.

Find creative ways to channel your own expression through whatever venue of art or business you desire. Here are some examples.

- *Dressing beautifully in bright, fun, flowy clothing.*
- *Accessorize with dangly costume jewelry and bold designs.*
- *Wear your hair in a feminine and sexy way.*
- *Design your own sacred spaces in your home or for others.*
- *Create anything you desire, such as a poem, painting, collage or other forms of mixed-media art.*

RECONNECTING TO CHILDHOOD WONDER AND CURIOSITY

"Wonder is the beginning of wisdom."
~Socrates

When we see the world the way we used to see it as children, as magical, beautiful, and filled with wonder, we return to the way we are meant to live every day. Children are open and always exploring the world through new eyes. They try new things, experiment and are always learning.

Children are pure and filled with curiosity for life. They see the world through a sense of amazement and wonder. They play and have fun with life. They don't overanalyze and worry.

__Invitation:__ Give yourself a set of new eyes. Take away everything you've been taught and see the subtle movements, colorful beauty and magic that you didn't see when you were caught up thinking so much. Let go of thought and look. What do you see?

HAPPINESS IS THE WAY TO HAPPINESS

"When I was 5 years old my mother always told me happiness was the key to life. When I went to school they asked me what I wanted to be when I grew up. I wrote down happy. They told me I didn't understand the assignment, and I told them they didn't understand life."
~John Lennon

We all want to be happy and live a good life, yet there are often blocks to us receiving and allowing true happiness in our lives. Currently western culture is constantly feeding us marketing messages telling us we aren't complete and whole unless we have this thing or that. In order for companies to make money off the old model, they disempower us into believing the latte will make us happy and then we need the perfect diet plan to look like the model in our favorite magazine. This happiness is external and all seeking through the outside world will never bring true happiness.

"Trying to be happy accumulating possessions is like trying to satisfy hunger by taping sandwiches all over your body."
~George Carlin

True happiness stems from our connection within and to truth. It begins with self love and results with healthy relationships, authentic friendships, loving families, community supports, joy, fun, purpose and pleasure.

When you live in a state of flow and trusting the universe has your back, you experience true happiness. You know how to flow and you trust that life isn't always going to be joyful in every moment. When we allow life to be life, we experience happiness. This is the source of true contentment.

I was always seeking happiness outside of myself, yet I found when I did that, I was never satisfied. It was never enough. The people, places and things usually did not fully satisfy me and if they did, a part of me rejected them, pushed them away. Why? Because deep inside I felt I didn't deserve it.

We can have everything we want on the outside. The perfect house, car, partner, kids, clothes, and so on. But if inside, we don't love ourselves, we won't really have those things and they won't last. Conversely, when we approach life from a place of gratitude and inner happiness, we naturally align with the higher vibration of gratitude and happiness. This is the law of attraction and that is what you naturally bring towards you, because that is what you are. Joy is the essence of success.

Invitation: Journal with the following phrase: "Happiness is..." Write whatever comes, resist the temptation to edit your words and just let it all flow out. This can be done with many feeling words.

BRIDGING ANCIENT SHAMANISM WITH THE MODERN WORLD

"In many shamanic societies, if you came to a medicine person complaining of being disheartened, dispirited, or depressed, they would ask one of four questions. When did you stop dancing? When did you stop singing? When did you stop being enchanted by stories? When did you stop finding comfort in the sweet territory of silence?
~Gabrielle Roth

Shamanism is an ancient practice of medicine, our ancestor's original medicine, that reunites us with the natural world for healing, renewal guidance and expansion. Many cultures, from the native people of Peru, Ireland, America and beyond still practice shamanism today and its influence is remerging at greater levels. Shamanism is about healing and renewing our connection with the natural world, including animals, plants and the land. It also helps us connect to our ancestors. Through the practice of shamanism, we can heal, receive answers to questions, access to guides, and greater clarity in life overall through accessing nature and other worlds of consciousness. This happens through the process of lucid dreaming and tapping into the four brain wave states of Beta (alertness and concentration), Alpha (creativity, relaxation and visualization), Theta (memory and intuition), and Delta (sleep and healing).

In the dream realm, accessed typically through guided imagery, drumming and/or rattling, a person is gently and safely guided out of ordinary reality into the lower, middle or upper worlds, where one can find access to helping spirits.

Helping spirits can include animal spirits and other guides, such as ancestors, angels and ascended masters.

Shamanism can also be used for the healing and reintegration of broken parts of the soul through the process of soul retrieval. The soul is whole naturally, but through certain life circumstances and traumas, we may have broken off or detached parts of ourselves that left in order to protect us at the time of the trauma. In essence those parts are always there, they may just have detached in one way or another. Soul retrieval is the act of undergoing a process where the conscious mind can rest and the subconscious mind can be accessed more readily in order to reunite the broken pieces back to the whole. This is not the only way, but it is one way to heal.

When shamans guide others into a shamanic journey, a person typically enters one of three worlds, the lower, upper and middle worlds. These three worlds are in non-ordinary reality. We leave ordinary reality to visit them. Usually the journeyer enters the lower or upper worlds in Shamanic journeying. These can be accessed through a dream-like state while still conscious and awake and it is often done with drumming and verbal cueing to help guide the journeyer.

The lower world is deep within the Earth and can be accessed through the base or roots of a tree, a hole in the ground, or through a doorway of any kind. It is where our animal spirit guide, all of the animal spirits and elemental realm, such as fairies, can be seen and communicated with more easily.

The middle world is similar to our world here now on Earth, just more vibrant and alive with color and beauty because we are often seeing differently in this state. When we access the middle world through the process of a shamanic journey, this may assist us in seeing our everyday world in ordinary reality from a new and heightened vision, the place of our Higher Self, rather than only our small or ego centered self. It is one way.

The upper world is that of the angelic realm, ascended masters, guides, and even loved ones who have passed. Through the practice of a shamanic journey, each of these worlds can be accessed to help us find answers to questions we are struggling with or just to understand something at deeper levels.

When I first heard about the practice of taking a shamanic journey into another world I was afraid. I asked questions like, "Where would I go? What if I get lost? What if I encounter danger? What if I don't come back?" My shamanic teacher calmed my fears and told me I would be safe, in control, and that she would guide me every step of the way. She said my soul travels during sleep and at other times and always knows where to return to my body. An energetic cord always connects my soul to my body. Trusting that and knowing everyone who has done this before has come back, I trusted her and laid down on the floor with blankets and pillows and listened to the sound of her drum. She led me through the journey through guided imagery and questions. I listened and allowed my experience to be what it was, without trying to make something happen. When I found myself trying to force something, I stepped back, knowing that if nothing came, that would be ok too. It was a restful and informative experience. I received answers to questions, solutions and clarity that I wasn't even seeking. I would definitely do it again and recommend it to others.

Invitation: *Discover more about shamanism and learn to connect to your primary spirit animal. Access can be made through taking a shamanic journey or possibly even asking for the answer to the question, "What is my primary spirit animal totem?" with a deck of spirit animal cards. My favorite teachers and authors on the topic of shamanism are Sandra Ingerman, Ted Andrews (1952-2009), and Dr. Stephen Farmer.*

Stacie Ivey

CHAPTER 9

CHAKRAS THROUGH THE ELEMENTAL GODDESSES

This is the realm of the Goddess. The chaos that comes in is meant to be here. The darkness fights harder to hold on the more the light shines upon it. This will continue for a while, and certain structures need to dissolve in order for beauty to rise, for beauty will rise.

The chakras are spinning vortexes of energy within our bodies. Our bodies are always vibrating and moving and are never still. It is now understood in the field of physics that everything is energy. As science continues to uncover new realms and dimensions of awareness, knowledge, wisdom and understanding that were once unknown, so must we continue to flow with these discoveries and teach them to our children.

There are seven primary energy centers coded within the body and although there are more being discovered; we will focus on seven in this book. If we see our bodies as a map, we can identify the seven primary chakras beginning with the feet and moving up through the tailbone, hips, solar plexus, heart, throat, third eye, and then the crown of head. The descriptions below blend the chakra system with the elemental energies and link them to the Divine Feminine Goddess energies.

Chakra 1–Earth Goddess and the Grounding Power of Earth

"How do the geese know when to fly to the sun? Who tells them the seasons? How do we humans, know when it is time to move on? As with the migrant birds, so surely with us, there is a voice within, if only we would listen to it, that tells us so certainly when to go forth into the unknown."
~Elisabeth Kubler Ross

The first chakra, Muladhara, the root chakra, is represented in the body by the tailbone, legs and feet. When we are feeling anxious, coming into the first chakra helps us feel grounded, safe and secure. Formation of the first chakra occurs in utero and through the first 6-12 months. Our experience in this stage of development informs the first chakra. For example, if in utero through your first year your mother was anxious, depressed, or if there was violence of any kind, you would have an increased likelihood of a wound (cellular memory) and imbalances in your first chakra.

1. **Balanced:** Feeling trustful, safe and secure in the world, especially around basic survival needs like food, shelter and money.
2. **Unbalanced:** Feeling anxious, restless, hoarding behaviors, gambling, shopping and food addictions, abandonment issues, and fear of not having enough money.

The first chakra is about our connection to Earth. When we don't feel connected to Earth, we aren't connected to our reality. We may want to be just spiritual, but it's also important to be grounded. Being grounded to the Earth is the way to connect more deeply to higher spiritual levels.

Nature has its own vibration and our body is in a natural alignment with that vibration. This is why nature feels so healing. When all else fails, nature has a way of bringing us back into the present moment and into our bodies, which are one with all of nature, including the physical plants, rocks, animals, as well as the spirits of the plants, rocks and animals.

Invitations:

- *To feel grounded, connect to your body from the waist down. Feel your feet on the floor and if you are sitting, your seat in the chair. Take a few deep breaths. Allow yourself to feel centered and close to the Earth.*
- *Spend time walking on the Earth in your bare feet.*
- *Try dancing in a drumming circle or taking an African dance class.*
- *Notice the three-dimensionality of nature.*
- *Pay attention to the vibrancy of colors and the texture of things in nature, such as in tree bark, rocks or leaves.*
- *Connect to an animal or insect and see what the characteristics of that animal or insect can teach you about life. For example, an eagle may help you see a situation from a more expansive and broader perspective.*
- *Grow your own food.*
- *Learn more about the Goddess Gaia.*
- *Learn more about and practice connecting to Archangel Uriel.*
- *Practice grounding yoga poses, such as mountain and Goddess poses.*
- *Find crystals that may help you feel grounded. Hematite and snowflake obsidian are good choices.*
- *Essential oils that can help the first chakra are cedarwood, basil, and patchouli.*

CHAKRA 2: WATER GODDESS AND THE HEALING POWER OF WATER

"Water is the mirror that has the ability to show us what we cannot see.
It is a blueprint for our reality, which can change with a single, positive
thought. All it takes is faith, if you're open to it."
~Masaru Emoto

The second chakra, Svadhishtana, the sacral chakra, is located in the hips, pelvis and sexual organs and develops between 12-18 months. It is linked to creation, birth, sensuality and our emotional identity. The second chakra is about our basic right to feel, explore and experience pleasure. As women, many of us have experienced some form of abuse in the area of this chakra, and in turn we cut ourselves off from the right to experience pleasure in whatever way we desire to experience it. There is guilt and shame connected to being the "good girl" as well as fear of truly allowing ourselves to be vulnerable. It's safer this way, however, it's also cutting us off from being able to fully experience life and whatever is unhealed will remain unhealed until we have the courage and readiness to face it. When we face it, the power it has over us is lessened and can even dissipate completely.

1. **Balanced:** Creative, explores life, enjoys the pleasures of life, and is comfortable in one's own sexuality.
2. **Unbalanced:** Sexual, alcohol and drug addictions, fear of exploring life, guilt and shame around pleasure and sexuality.

Many of the energetic wounds or imbalances we carry in the second chakra are often not even ours. We could be carrying that which belonged not to us but rather to our mothers, grandmothers, ancestors or even other lifetimes. The reality is that we are multidimensional beings, but whatever is unhealed, no matter the source, it can be healed and released now.

As women, we are emotional beings and in touch with our emotions more often than men. Culturally, we weren't taught how to deal with uncomfortable emotions and because our emotions aren't always "pretty," we have a tendency to embrace only the "good" emotions and resist the "bad" ones. Rather, when we embrace all of our emotions, we recognize that emotions flow through a large spectrum of heights, dips and all the places in between, and it's all part of the experience of being human. The more we allow our emotions to be what they are, without resistance, the more easily they can flow through us the same way water flows. Emotions are simply energy in motion. It is not the emotion, but our thoughts and judgments about emotion that causes suffering.

The second chakra is where women manifest their creative projects in the world. It begins from the bottom up and is a powerful place of creation, not only for birthing physical children but anything that wants to be created through women, such as a new business, book, painting, or any creative project.

As the element of the second chakra, water is integral to life and can teach us so much. It is both soft and powerful. It is elusive, meaning it is as hard to hold onto as if you tried to hold water in your hands. Like water, it can be extremely soft, allowing us to sit in a warm bath and be rejuvenated after a long day, and it can also destroy mountains, cities and life. It both nourishes and destroys life. Water is full of paradoxes, just as is life.

When we take ourselves into water we feel free and more alive. We connect to the playfulness of water and our inner child awakens. Water reminds us of the life force that is water flowing through our veins and arteries, up to our heart in the form of blood.

Water is profoundly healing and essential to our wellbeing. The human body is made up of primarily water, and we need water both internally and externally to survive, thrive and heal. When we give ourselves over to water, it cleanses negative energy off of us. We can allow water to wash away whatever we feel we are holding onto. Water cleanses the electrical energy systems of our bodies and brings us back into a state of balance.

"You are not a drop in the ocean, but the entire ocean in a drop."
~Rumi

Invitations:

- **River:** *Rather than always trying to swim upstream with a lot of effort, feeling like you have to do and figure it all out yourself, just get on the raft and flow with the river.*

- **Pond:** *Reflect upon how a lotus flower begins at the bottom of a pond, growing in the darkness, muck and mud, and rises up through the water into a beautiful creation. It is through the darkness that we can rise up and cleanse away the muck to reveal the true beauty and light within.*

- **Ocean:** *Think of the expansive depth of the ocean. Imagine that you are one with the ocean.*

- *Connect to your inner mermaid: Play and have fun with life.*

- **Falling Water:** *Allow rain, a waterfall or a shower to wash away the burdens and fears that hold you back and keep you stuck in your small self. Open to the possibilities of who and what you truly are, which is one with the Divine. When you open to that understanding, you are unlimited.*

- **Bathing:** *Take an amazing bath in Epsom salts and feel the healing of effects of water. When you're finished sitting, you can drain the water while you* *remain sitting in the water. During the process of the water draining, imagine all of the emotional, physical and energetic weights you've been carrying around to go down the drain as well. The water is a healer, cleanser and carrier.*

- *Visit a natural hot spring area.*
- *Take a belly dancing class.*
- *Learn more about the Goddess Eurynome.*
- *Learn more about and practice connecting to Archangel Jophiel.*
- *Yoga poses that can help include cat/ cow, pigeon, frog, and goddess poses.*
- *Crystals to balance the second chakra include citrine, carnelian and fire opal.*
- *Essential oils for chakra two are tangerine, orange, and cinnamon.*

CHAKRA 3-FIRE GODDESS AND THE TRANSFORMATIVE POWER OF FIRE

"Be who you were created to be and you will set the world on fire."
~St. Catherine of Siena

Manipura chakra is the third chakra, which sits within the solar plexus (core) and directly links us to the element of fire. This chakra is responsible for standing in our power and owning our place in the world and develops between 18-42 months. The solar plexus chakra's focus is empowered living and bringing forth who you are meant to become in this lifetime.

Fire is a powerful transformational tool. The transformational nature of fire can be seen in the sun shining down and the resultant metamorphosis of the Earth below, volcanos deconstructing the land when they blow, sweat, and the fire in our belly as we digest our food. Additionally, fire is the catalyst for the alchemy of transformation, turning lead into gold or whatever needs to be released so the brilliance beneath can shine.

In yoga, there are samskaras. These are the imprints we carry around of false energy, hurts and beliefs that don't serve us but haven't yet healed. Through the energy of fire, sweat and awareness, samskaras can be burned away for your true essence to shine.

1. **Balanced:** Strong sense of self-confidence, knowing you are here for a reason and purpose, and feeling comfortable shining your own unique light in the world.
2. **Unbalanced:** Feeling ashamed, crouching inward, fear of being seen, not knowing who you are.

Invitation:

- *What do you want to transform in your life?*
- *Where can you own your power in an area of your life more? Consider your health, romantic partners, friends, spirituality, and emotional health.*
- *Create a positive affirmation related to this aspect you'd like to transform and place it somewhere you will see it a lot. Read it daily.*
- *Learn more about the Goddess Pele.*
- *Learn more about and practice connecting to Archangel Michael.*
- *Yoga poses for power include the warrior poses and triangle pose.*
- *Crystals to balance chakra three are amber, citrine, and sunstone.*
- *Essential oils for the third chakra include clove, ginger, grapefruit, and wintergreen.*

CHAKRA 4-LOVE GODDESS AND THE TRANSCENDENT POWER OF LOVE

"Love is the bridge between you and everything."
~Rumi

The fourth chakra, Anahata, is located within the heart and associated with the element of air. Anahata connects us to the power of love. It develops between three and a half and seven years and is linked to our joy, social identity, relationships, and right to give and receive love. Anahata sits at the center point of our bodies and is the only horizontal axis of the seven chakras, which connects the bottom three, Earth, to the top three, heaven, creating heaven on Earth within our bodies. When we connect to unconditional love, all possibilities become available to us and the world can literally shift immediately from fear to love. Love is the truth of who we are and fear is an illusion.

1. **Balanced:** Healthy and balanced relationships, ability to love oneself, and the ability to give and receive love freely.
2. **Unbalanced:** Co-dependency, love addictions, addictions to sugar and smoking

The fourth chakra's element is air. Air carries the life force energy or prana that flows through us, sustaining us and keeping us alive through our breath. Our breath flows in and out of our lungs as regulated by the cerebellum, just as the wind blows through the trees and across the Earth as regulated by the atmospheric shifts on the planet. When we connect to the element of air, we connect to love, ease of movement, change, dreams taking flight and freedom.

Invitation: *Try these tools to enhance the fourth chakra:*

- *Look in the mirror, smile and saying positive things to yourself, such as "I love you."*
- *Think of someone you love unconditionally and give that same gift of love to yourself.*
- *Do something physical to raise your heartbeat and then feel the pulsating beat of your heart.*
- *Learn more about the Goddess Aphrodite.*
- *Learn more about and practice connecting to Archangel Raphael.*
- *Practice restorative yoga and yoga nidra. Consider heart opening poses, such as fish and camel.*
- *Crystals to balance the heart chakra are rose quartz, smoky quartz, emerald, and malachite.*
- *Essential oils to help your heart connection include rose, geranium, ylang ylang, peppermint, eucalyptus, and lime.*

CHAKRA 5-TRUTH GODDESS AND THE POWER OF SPEECH AND WORDS

"Every word you utter to another human being has an effect. But you don't know it."
~Howard Zinn

Chakra five, Vishuddhi, is located in the throat and is the home of speaking of truth and the power of our speech and words. It develops between ages seven and twelve and the element associated with Vishuddhi is sound.

1. **Balanced:** Being able to speak truth freely and fearlessly
2. **Unbalanced:** Lies, fear of rejection around speaking truth, smoking addictions, throat cancer.

When we feel empowered with our speech, we say what we need to say without fear of judgment or abandonment. We stand in our truth and are willing to risk the other person not liking what they hear. This is the power of words because they carry coding and vibrational messages that have a powerful effect on us. In Shamanic cultures, words are things. We have the power to create our reality, call upon spiritual assistance and heal with words. In recognition of the power of words, we must use them wisely. Certain words carry low vibrational frequencies, such as hate and disgust, and other words carry high vibrational frequencies, such as love and peace.

You will know a truly wise person by the number of words they use. A fool will use a lot of words and repeat themselves over and over again so they can be seen and heard. A wise person observes and only says what needs to be said. When a wise person speaks, each word has value and carries with it an energy of presence, rather than an energy of desperation or neediness.

Speaking our truth is not always an easy task. In the song by John Mayer, "Say what you need to say," we are reminded to speak our truth even when we are afraid and even when it is difficult. We may be afraid to speak our truth because we are afraid of being rejected and getting hurt. This is likely because at a certain point in our past life experiences, we had the experience of abandonment, on varying degrees and levels, as a result of our speaking truth.

Invitation:

- *Say what you need to say, but release yourself from the outcome and expectations.*
- *Practice the mantra, either verbally or thinking the phrase "so hum". So (inhale) hum (exhale) and repeat for as long as needed.*
- *Learn more about the Goddess Iris.*
- *Learn more about and practice connecting to Archangel Gabriel.*
- *Crystals to help with the fifth chakra are lapis lazuli, angelite, celestite, turquoise, and aquamarine.*
- *Essential oils beneficial for opening the throat charka are jasmine, geranium, peppermint and eucalyptus.*

CHAKRA 6-INTUITIVE GODDESS: THE THIRD EYE AND INTUITION

"The intuitive mind is a sacred gift and the rational mind is a faithful servant. We have created a society that honors the servant and has forgotten the gift."
~Albert Einstein

The sixth chakra, Ajna, is located in the brow, associated with the element of light, and develops during puberty. Ajna is responsible for intuition, wisdom, imagination, focus, clarity, and visualization.

1. **Balanced:** Trusting that inner guidance and wisdom is real, paying attention to synchronicities.
2. **Unbalanced:** Anxious, fearful, not trusting in the world, feeling disconnected from life.

Intuition is largely misunderstood and beyond time and space. Eastern cultures have always known about the power of the third eye and one's intuition. Yet in the West, intuition has been discounted as a new-age concept or simply ignored completely.

> *Before studying yoga, I had no idea the third eye existed. I remember seeing women from India with the dot on their forehead, but had no idea why they had that and what it was for. Now I know the importance of that dot. It reminds the women to never forget their intuition. It reminds them to see through their spiritual, or third eye, which sees far more that what we can see through our limited two physical eyes.*

So, what is intuition?

Intuition is our inborn gift. It is the voice of the true self, our higher self, the self that is connected to all and never dies. Intuition is the voice of our soul. It tells us when to stop and when to go and guides us to take one path over another. Intuition is a quiet, still voice that speaks to us. We all have the ability to see, hear, feel or know beyond the realm of the physical. There are four metaphysical (beyond the physical) senses that supplement our five physical senses of sight, hearing, taste, smell and touch. They give practical and helpful information for finding out information and keeping us safe. Everyone has access to these intuitive gifts, but as each of us are unique, we may have strengths more in some and less in others. As with anything, it only takes training, tools, and practice to develop them. They include:

CLAIRSENTIENCE — CLEAR FEELING

Clairsentience is the ability to feel energy. It is the sense that something is present that cannot be seen and yet it is felt it in some way. This can also occur when an uncomfortable feeling arises around a certain person or in a certain place. Clairsentience is the gift of intuition telling the truth, which often our logical mind wants to discount. Clairsentience is the sense that gives a bad feeling when someone is dangerous to be around or it tells us to leave an environment that isn't good to be in.

CLAIRVOYANCE — CLEAR SEEING

Clairvoyance is the ability to see energy. Individuals with the gift of clairvoyance are called clairvoyants and can see a variety of energies, including, auras, colors, spiritual beings, guides, angels, ancestors, loved ones who have passed, and even the elemental (Earth spirit) realm of fairies and unicorns. Some clairvoyants will see all of the above and even more and others will see only some of the above. Fortunately, it is not a competition and those who can "see" recognize it for the gift that it is.

CLAIRAUDIENCE — CLEAR HEARING

Clairaudience is the ability to hear beyond the ears. Often we get stuck in the belief that if we don't hear it with our physical ears, it doesn't exist. That leaves out so much of the world. Just because we don't hear it, does it mean it doesn't exist? Obviously that could be debated. What about the hearing of dogs and other animals? Do they hear differently or more than us? Maybe we will never know. Clairaudience is the ability to pick up audible information energetically. It allows us access to the energetic realm of hearing, beyond the physical ears.

Those who have tapped into and can access the spiritual gift of clairaudience can hear energies, guides, deceased loved ones, or helping spirits through messages that come into the ear energetically.

CLAIRCOGNIZANCE — CLEAR KNOWING

Claircognizance is the ability to know messages from the spirit world. It's the acceptance of when you "just know" something is about to happen or has happened. It's when you get an intuitive "hit" that tells you information about a person, place, thing, or event that you wouldn't otherwise know about.

At first, when you begin to realize you even have an instinct that is guiding you, it is difficult to discern whether or not what you are listening to is your own voice or the voice of your higher self, angels, guides, Spirit, God, or whatever other name you want to use. Finding it for yourself is key, and identifying what is comfortable for you is where the wisdom lies. This is not about trying to impose my beliefs or will onto you, it is about empowering you to listen to your own inner wisdom, the place you find yourself. When you know, you just know.

There was a time in my life when I was given that small still voice that told me to leave, rather than sit in a situation where I was manipulated and lied to and about to sign off on a legal document that wasn't in alignment with my values. The voice said, don't sign it, just go, but I didn't listen, which resulted in 18 months of intense suffering, followed by a huge wakeup call that I was either going to listen to and regain my power or not listen to and die. It was that straightforward. It was that simple. Death seemed like the better option, especially in the darkest moments, but instead I chose life.

Because the voice of our intuition is subtle, still and quiet, it can be difficult to hear when you are distracted by the outside world. Think of a casino. The reason a casino is so loud and distracting is because it keeps us from tuning into which machine will pay out or which card to play in that moment. Intuition comes in strongly when we are quiet and distraction free, when we are able to go within. The voice of intuition comes from within. It communicates differently than the mind and is difficult to translate at first.

When we are in a place of fear and don't know what to decide, it's hard to know whether what we think we should do is coming from a place of the mind/ego or intuition/soul. Our logical mind, which is primarily in our brain's left hemisphere, has been so conditioned that we don't trust the small, still voice within. We may feel a little pull in one direction, but don't listen to it because the logical part of our mind tells us we can't do that or it doesn't make sense.

What I have learned is that when you get a "hit" and it's immediate, such as needing to get away from a situation, person, place or thing, you should listen to it.

Other situations are more difficult because they don't require an immediate decision, even though we may be feeling pressure to decide right there and then. In those situations, when it's not life or death, usually you can take some time. Take a day. Remove yourself from needing to decide and sleep on it. Go within. The easiest times to go within, especially when you're "new" to it, is to do some movement first, like dancing around the room or practicing yoga. Another way is to listen to a guided meditation or practice Japa meditation, which is a spiritual practice using a mantra (a word or phrase, in Sanskrit or English), often paired with a mala necklace (108-beaded necklace) to quiet the mind and go more easily within. All of these techniques help calm the mind and take it from a place of fear into the body and into the present moment. When you go into the body, it's much easier to listen to the voice of the soul.

Invitation:
  * *Think of a time when you were given an opportunity to listen to your own small, still voice within and didn't listen. What were the ramifications of that choice? Now step back from that and view it from a*

*place of non-judgment, compassion and forgiveness.
Come back to this moment. Know that you did the
best you knew at the time and use this experience as
an opportunity to learn from. When you know
better, do better. It's all going to be okay. It already
is. The key is to see beyond the illusions. See life as
unlimited, ever changing and transformational.*

- *Practice enhancing your imagination. Tune into the
  place between your eyebrows and close your eyes.
  Imagine going somewhere you've never been or
  dreaming of something you wish for in your life.*
- *Learn more about the Goddess Saraswati.*
- *Learn more about and practice connecting to
  Archangel Haniel.*
- *Crystals to help with the sixth chakra are lapis
  lazuli and blue quartz.*
- *Essential oils that balance the third eye chakra
  include clary sage and lemongrass.*

CHAKRA 7–SPIRIT GODDESS: THE CROWN AND CHANNELING UP

Travel light, live light, spread the light, be the light.
~Yogi Bhajan

The seventh chakra is located at the top of the head,
associated with the element of thought and develops after
puberty, although the children being born now already have
this awareness, whether they can communicate it or not. It is
associated with consciousness, realization, grace, selflessness
and oneness.

We are always in communion with spirit, whether we
know it or not. At the level of the seventh chakra, there is no

separateness, only union, and we realize we are a direct channel to the Divine. At this level of conscious awareness, we see beyond the senses and open to the language of spirit. The crown chakra is the level of angels, spiritual guides, ascended masters and the universe. We forget that we are never alone and are loved unconditionally, always. The world we live in is very distracting and keeps us disconnected from our source. Religion from the past has had an impact on this, such as in the Catholic church.

Growing up Catholic, I was taught that the only direct connection we had to God was through a priest, to whom we had to confess our sins. I never felt I had a direct connection to God and never even heard of Goddess being spoken in church, other than Mother Mary, who was never referred to a Goddess, but rather the mother of God. As a child, I remember getting traumatized with butterflies in my stomach over going into the confessional and hoping I remembered all of my sins, which were mostly not being as kind as I could have been to my brother, which created internal shame.

The first time I remember being told about my angels, I was a child and was told I had a guardian angel. I thank God for my grandmother, a beautiful woman who aged so well no one could believe she was 95, when she looked no older than 75. She believed in angels and had many angel figurines around her home. Since everyone knew she believed in angels, that's what everyone bought her. She loved angels. Growing up, angels were more of a concept to me. I believed in them, but didn't have anything to relate to other than the mini statues in my grandmother's home and a few pictures I had seen. The picture that stands out the most to me is the image of the guardian angel over the boy and girl child. My grandmother had that image in her home and even found me a nightlight of that image. As an adult, I remember being told by an angel reader who would draw the angels she saw in someone's aura that I had two angels who were always with me and they were frustrated that I don't listen to them, but they love me very much. That was reassuring to me and the first time I felt I could get closer to them and connect to them more deeply.

Invitation: *Try using these tools to enhance your connection to the seventh chakra.*

- *Consistent daily meditation.*
- *Learn more about the Goddess Sophia.*
- *Learn more about and practice connecting to Archangel Metatron.*
- *Yoga poses that are inversions, especially those that compress and release the crown, such as rabbit pose and headstand.*
- *Crystals to help with the seventh chakra are amethyst, sapphire, and diamond.*
- *Essential oils that are beneficial include frankincense, lemon, Melissa, rosemary and chamomile.*

Stacie Ivey

PART 3

Sacred Expansion

"Once, when you thought no one was looking, I saw you open your heart so wide that the Earth fell in. Once, when you thought no one was listening, I heard you sigh so deep that the oceans roared with support. Once, when you thought no one was around, every atom in this universe rushed forward to embrace you. Again. Thank you for existing so intensely."

~Sera Beak

Stacie Ivey

When the Sacred Mother beholds you, there is only beauty.

She is patient and waits compassionately.

A peace overcomes and surrounds you that allows for no more fear.

Fear is simply a part of the ego which is meant to help keep you alive, but not take over your life.

Have you temporarily forgotten your spiritual self?

Have you temporarily forgotten the realm of the sacred?

When you enter this realm, nothing else that matters.

All fears dissipate.

You are held and loved unconditionally, the way you always wished for and wanted from your own mother.

In this lifetime, your mother may or may not have been able to give you what you needed. She was only able to give what she had, stemming from what she was given or not given from her own mother. She carried wounds and pain herself.

Yet, in the realm of the Divine Mother, you are held with such sacred beauty and unconditional love that holds you so closely, you suddenly realize you have nothing to fear.

Her love for you is so powerful, strong and unwavering. You are loved not for what you do or don't do, but simply for who you are.

Her love is unconditional and you are held in this love now and always.

Stacie Ivey

CHAPTER 10

SACRED SEXUALITY

"It is time we saw sex as the truly sacred art that it is. A deep meditation, a holy communion, and a dance with the force of creation.."
~Marcus Allen

A woman's sexuality, when empowered and fully in her choice, is sensual, erotic, beautiful and sacred. She is in her power and she radiates a power and light that is through and of the Divine. She is juicy, vibrant and magnetic. First she must recognize this possibility, heal the wounds hidden in her womb, and then open to the beauty of the experience of receiving the gifts her sexuality has for her, whether she wants to experience it through a single partner or through the direct connection she has with the Divine in any other way she chooses.

THE SACRED WOMB

"The womb is a living metaphor for your transformation."
~Aadma and Anaiya Aon Prakasha in "Womb Wisdom"

The womb is a powerful place of connection for women, and this knowledge is life-changing for not only women, but also men. Men also carry a womb space, not in the same physical way as women, but energetically. When both women and men understand this power, respecting it fully as the gift it is, this realization alone can change the world.

For many years there has been a strong disempowerment for women through a disconnection from their sensuality, sexuality and the power of manifestation women carry in their womb space. The womb holds the energy of water and is connected to the second chakra. When women learn to reconnect to their womb space, love it and embody it fully and completely, they are powerful change agents in the world. Women have the power to make catalytic shifts in the consciousness of the world through this reconnection that was lost over time.

Starting before, but especially since the advent of the Catholic Church and the dominance of the masculine energy and ideals, there has been a system in place that feared the power of women. There was a desire for power and control and it was discovered that repressing women's sensuality and sexuality would be the way to overpower the masses. When women have power, all thrive and a utopian world is possible. When there is an imbalance of power, there is destruction, fighting, anger, hatred, animosity and a world that represses, segregates and separates people. This is the world we live in right now, but there is a profound and amazing movement starting that is coming from within us, women especially.

Women are feeling the call within them to bring forth a new world, and the energy that exists on the planet right now is full of infinite possibilities.

Invitation: *Recognize the powerful magnetic presence that comes from being connected to your womb space. Breathe it in and feel it fully. As you access its power, you create the life of your dreams. Try this guided imagery:*

- *Tune into your womb space.*
- *Place your hands on your lower abdomen. Your thumbs will touch at your belly button and your fingers will point down with the tips of your index fingers touching. All four fingers just rest side by side normally, creating an upside down triangle opening between your two hands.*
- *Breathe into your womb. Take a deep inhale. Take a deep exhale.*
- *Do this a couple more times, breathing as deeply and slowly as you can.*
- *Let your body relax and if you feel comfortable, close your eyes.*
- *Imagine your womb as if it were a bowl.*
- *What does it look like?*
- *Does it have anything noticeable about it?*
- *What does it feel like?*
- *Continue to breathe and accept whatever you observe, just as it is.*
- *Now, imagine your womb being filled with a golden or pink light.*
- *Imagine it being nourished and healed.*
- *Let this light heal all the areas where it felt incomplete, hurt or broken.*
- *Now imagine someone or something you want to bring into your life. This could be a new partner, a child, book, or business. Whatever you desire, imagine it.*
- *Place the image of what you desire into your womb space and hold it there.*
- *Take three deep breaths with this image, knowing your womb is the place where all is birthed into the world.*
- *Carry this with you and sit until you feel ready to open your eyes and return to the world.*
- *Consider doing practice often and see what happens. You can return to it anytime.*

Returning to erotic
sensuality

*"The body is an instrument which only gives off music when it is used
as a body. Always an orchestra, and just as music transverses walls, so
sensuality transverses the body and reaches up to ecstasy."*

~Anais Nin

When we view our bodies as a sacred and erotic creations, we can open to more fully enjoying the pleasures of our bodies. This means allowing the raw, juicy and naked parts of us to come out in the most primal and unlimited sense. As we allow ourselves to feel this completely, we experience true bliss and freedom.

Conversely, this allowance is extremely vulnerable and the reason we cut ourselves off from experiencing pleasure and the Divine human experience without guilt or fear. Throughout history women have been objectified and misused in one form or another. Women have been seen as objects and have in turn used the power of their bodies to overcompensate for the abuse and neglect by manipulating men through their sexuality. This is the dark side or shadow of sex being misused by women. Women can have a tendency to either fear their sexuality and repress it or overuse their sexuality and manipulate with it. Neither are pretty and the balance comes first in recognizing and healing the past hurts and wounds. Often the crimes to women's bodies have been done by men, but not always. Often the womb, which is the most powerful component of a woman for manifestation and creation of her dreams, is muffled or blocked due to past traumas and abuse.

Invitations:

- *Imagine for a moment that you are a beautiful crystal wine glass and you are awaiting the most amazing, highest-quality wine that exists on this planet made from organic grapes. You are open to receiving the best, most amazing wine to come into you and give you the most tantalizing and tasteful glass of classy exotic and erotic wine that exists on the planet. How would you be in the world if you treated yourself the way you would savor, explore and cherish that glass of wine.*

- *Now consider that Source energy is your Divine lover. Tap into the infinite, ecstatic, and abundant love that loves for the sake of love. It is juicy, sexy, sacred, and pure all at the same time.*
- *Explore all of your senses.*
- *Allow yourself to slow down.*
- *Try tantric practices alone or with a partner.*

BIRTH

"We have a secret in our culture, it's not that birth in painful, it's that women are strong."
~Laura Stavoe Harm

Everything that exists on this planet, whether it is people, plants, animals, businesses, structures, or systems has gone through a transition from the invisible to visible, from darkness to light. This is the process of birth. All that exists here in this world has been birthed in one way or another through creation. The world we live in is in duality. It is the design of the Earth that both darkness and light exist together. We are here to birth the light into all things, whether it be through our children, our businesses or ourselves. We are all meant to heal and to recognize our wholeness. It is only through birth that we can do this.

It is through the darkness that all things are born. Think of an infant in a mother's womb. It is in darkness for a period of time and then it is born into the light of the world. In business, all ideas spark from the light of an inspiration or thought that was once in the darkness and is now brought forth into light.

Ideas that come from the place of inspiration are different from those born in thought. In thought, the solutions may be coming from a place of effort or a limited way of viewing the solution to a problem. This is where something may seem like a good idea at the time, but over time it reveals itself as something that needs adjustment or change. Change is the only thing that can be counted on. We are always in a constant state of change, whether we see it or not. Know that birth is taking place always. You are birthing new aspects of you, internally and externally, as you grow and expand at all times.

Invitation: *Consider that all creativity or "birthing" comes from the Divine, Source energy, and God/Goddess. We are simply channels to inspiration, which comes from Spirit through us. All we need to do is allow, open and put ourselves in situations that open the doors for creativity to come through more easily. This can be accessed many ways, such as going for a walk in nature, doing yoga, listening to inspiring music, or simply putting a paintbrush to a canvas and seeing what happens. When inspiration hits, it is often unexpected. Write it down and follow through. That is your responsibility because you were "chosen" with the idea. Otherwise, you wouldn't have been given the idea. The idea was given by God/Goddess to you to bring into the physical world. It is a gift as you are a gift.*

HONORING THE SEASONS, CYCLES AND CHANGES WITHIN OUR BODIES AND IN NATURE

"Seasons of waiting are designed to prepare you, stretch your faith and get you ready for everything that's coming next."
~Mandy Hale

Nature is cyclical. Look at the seasons. Spring is a time of planting and new beginnings. Summer is a time of fun and color. Fall is the harvest and winter is the going within.

Additionally, for women, the moon cycle is a reminder of the natural cycles and rhythms of your body. Most women who grew up in Western culture were fed the ideas that her period is gross, a burden, and another way to reject her body.

Our ancestors bled in rhythm with the moon and were deeply connected to nature and space. They had awareness that they came from the stars and they honored the moon and the deep and profound wisdom of their bodies. They celebrated the gifts of their body and life.

> **Invitation:** *Consider that your moon cycle is a powerful opportunity to go within, listen at deeper levels and acknowledge our deep connection to all things. Listen. The wisdom of your higher self, angels, guides or anything connected to the Goddess are easier to hear when you get quiet.*

Stacie Ivey

CHAPTER 11

RECEPTIVITY

"I am not my thoughts, emotions, sense perceptions and experiences.
I am not the content of my life.
I am life.
I am the space in which all things happen.
I am consciousness.
I am the Now.
I Am."
~ Eckhart Tolle

Receptivity is the way of the feminine. It is about tapping into our intuition and trusting our gut instinct. We have been taught we must do and achieve in order to live fulfilled lives, but for women, this depletes our energy and turns us into men in women's bodies. The way of the woman is to be penetrated with beauty, Divine inspiration and gifts that are meant for us so that we will share them with the world, whether it be in our immediate families or on a larger scale with groups, communities and globally. The more we can learn to receive, the more we can give back to others.

Synchronicities are Everywhere

"Synchronicity happens when you align with the universe rather than insisting the universe flow your way."
~The Akashic Records

Synchronicities are a way of letting us know we're on the right track. They are a literal pat on the back from the Divine, telling us to keep going in that direction, sort of like flowing with the river rather than swimming upstream.

> *I have just had the experience of not trusting myself, which is something I have chosen to replay in my experience over and over. This is because I wasn't fully acknowledging it and it needed to be seen. When I was a child, my mother always made me question my decisions so I would blindly follow hers. So I began and kept playing the story of "I can't trust myself," over and over. When I decided it was time, I chose to stop telling myself the same story. I could make the choice. This is where empowerment comes in. I could choose to be empowered or I could tell myself the opposite, "I can trust myself." Whichever one I chose to believe is the one that became true for me. It was that simple.*

We grew up with the conditioning that this wasn't true. We grew up believing we can't manifest our dreams. That just isn't true. It is actually a big fat lie.

There was a truth that I spoke out loud the other day. It was a truth that I always knew about myself, yet didn't always think about. However, because it was planted as a seed in my subconscious, it was leading the way. The truth was this:

> *I am getting messages all the time from spirit, but sometimes I don't trust them.*

I said that truth out loud after I heard it being spoken by my husband. I heard it differently then, in a new way, and I let it percolate for a while. At the moment I said that truth out loud, I was driving and passed an instant rainbow coming magically toward my car in the street. It was a rainbow being made from the sprinklers watering the grass at the expansive community park across the street from my home. It was an affirmation. It was quick and subtle, and I didn't doubt it. The spiritual journey is one in which we may think, "Once I reach a certain point of enlightenment, then I won't suffer, then I won't have to work anymore at this spiritual enlightenment stuff.

That is another illusion. It is the mind telling us a lie. It is a process. You move forward and sometimes you may fall back a little, but each time, coming back is a little easier. The more you practice, the more it becomes effortless. It is just like learning anything new, such as a sport, or yoga. You keep coming back to the practice. You keep on the path. It is about the journey, not the destination. It is like riding the waves of the ocean. You have ups and you have downs. The key is to remain steady. The key is to recognize your triggers. With practice, the triggers lessen. With practice, the storms calm. With practice, you begin to realize all is well.

So with "practice," what is it that I am referring to? It could be meditation, yoga, mindfulness, spending time in nature, or creating art. It could be everything and nothing. The key is to find what works for you. The key is to listen to your guidance and pay attention to your synchronicities and to do the work, even if you don't feel like it. If we waited until we felt like it, we would never get anything done. Action is so important.

"Just do it."
~Nike slogan

Invitation: *Allow what wants to come through you to come and then take action when you feel you are being called to take action. Allow it to manifest in perfect form. Trust that all is well, because it is.*

OPENING TO SYNCHRONICITIES

"Don't dismiss the synchronicity of what is happening right now finding its way to your life at this moment. There are no coincidences in the universe, only convergences of will, intent, and experience."
~Neale Donald Walsch

There is an amazing magic that we become aware of the more we open to and trust the realm of Spirit. I once had a spiritual teacher tell me, "Synchronicities are happening all the time, it's just whether or not we are paying attention."

Here is a personal example of a synchronicity I experienced: There was a fee I had to pay that was a large sum, in the amount of $1680.00. I wasn't sure how I was going to pay it, other than I knew I had a little bit of money in my business account. I had typically been a worrier my whole life, but this time I didn't worry. I just knew what I needed would be brought to me, I just didn't know how. Well, here's how it happened. First, I checked my business account and discovered I had $900 in it that I could pull out. Then, a few days later, my husband and I had to return a television we had recently purchased and weren't going to use. The store returned us the money in the amount of $680 in cash! I hadn't fully realized I had all the money I needed until I counted what was in the envelope and discovered I had $1580. I was $100 dollars short on the day I was going to pay the bill and thought I had the money in my wallet, but I didn't. I had remembered my husband had handed me $100 the other day, but it wasn't in my wallet. I couldn't remember where the money had gone, so I calmed down and trusted the answer would be given to me. Then I remembered the red ski vest I had worn the day he

218

*handed me the $100 when I didn't have my wallet on me.
Was the money in my pocket? That's the guidance I was
given, so I checked and guess what! The entire remaining
amount of $100 was in my pocket. That is an example of
synchronicity.*

Invitation: *Pay attention to the unexpected events that occur
in your life, as if by magic, especially when you're trusting
God. Let go and let God. Journal about your experiences.
You will likely be surprised.*

BLESSINGS

"What seems to us as bitter trials are often blessings in disguise."
~Oscar Wilde

There is an abundance of blessings in the world, yet we don't
see them. We see some of them when we stop and notice,
when we are present. Yet, everything is a blessing. Everything
is a gift.

We notice blessings when we are in a place of gratitude.
When we are thankful for what we have and focus on our
blessings in life, rather than on our pain and lack, we are
gifted more blessings. Masters have taught this over time, yet
we live in a world where it's often not talked about. We live in
the most abundant time ever on our planet, yet carry around a
mentality of lack. We are told by advertisers trying to sell us
goods and services that we will be whole, complete, and
better if we have more, yet the truth is that we are whole and
complete just as we are. That's the irony. We are fed
information everywhere that is telling us we need more, when
we are enough. We have enough. What we need more of is
not things, but rather love. When we recognize the love
within ourselves and in each of us, we open to grace, which is
intertwined with blessings. Blessings are sacred mysteries that
cannot be explained.

When you experience them, you know them and you want to do whatever it takes to experience them again. They are the calling forth of the truth within each of us. They are beyond words and can only be explained through personal experiences and teachings.

As we are evolving out of a world that has been ruled by the mind, we step into grac and a bounty of the blessings that have always been present but often not seen. They are part of never-ending, always-flowing, abundant, unconditional love. If we lived with this full realization, there would only be gratitude and praise for the gifts and blessings in our life. There would only be God.

Everything is possible, and the pull toward this love is getting stronger. It is calling us to come closer, to notice, to wake up and to be here now. It is the force that is and always has been. It has never left and never will leave. As the words of Meister Eckhart so wisely state, "If the only prayer you ever say in your whole life is thank you, that would suffice."

Invitation: Notice your breath. Your breath is a blessing. It is the life force flowing through you, in and out of your lungs and oxygenating all cells in your body. In yoga it is called prana and in Chinese medicine it is called chi. It doesn't matter what word we call it, all that matters is that we recognize the sacredness of it, the beauty and grace in it and the mystery of it all.

MIRACLES

"A miracle is a shift in perception from fear to love."
~A Course in Miracles

We are in a Divine play of form and everything in life is a miracle. No matter how it presents itself, watch the dynamics of human life. When we open to the fact that all of life is a miracle, we experience the miraculous nature of life. It is amazing on so many levels and beyond words. Life is found in the little moments, the small interactions as well as the big ones. When we learn to appreciate each moment, we begin to see the miracles of life in new and profound ways. Life becomes more animated, colorful, and alive. We block ourselves from life when we are afraid and asleep, or in other words, unconscious while awake. When we fully wake from the dream and see the miracle of life within the dream, an entirely new world and reality presents itself to us.

The way we see miracles depends on our beliefs.
Everyone is entitled to miracles.
Miracles occur naturally.

SACRED DEVOTION

"Acknowledging the good that you already have in your life is the foundation for all abundance."
~Eckhart Tolle

When we open our hearts to the abundance and totality of this life and all of the gifts within this life that are given to us, we can do nothing other than be grateful beyond words to the point of tears from the most profound realization of these gifts. The experience of this devotion is an experience of love at its highest levels and the more we open, the more capacity we have to receive this love. It is fruitful and abundant beyond anything we can even imagine.

Invitation: *Here are some ways to practice your personal devotion:*
- *Prayer*
- *Singing praise*
- *Creating a sacred space to spend time with the Divine*

- *Performing sacred rituals (see Chapter 9: The practice of rituals)*
- *Performing sacred ceremony, along the lines of what you may have observed in church, at a wedding or other rite of passage. The ceremony can range from simple to complex. Within a ceremony can be speaking a prayer, setting a verbal intention, calling in angels or guides, asking to be surrounded in light and protection, lighting a candle or cleansing a room, home or any space with a sage stick.*
- *Having regular and consistent sacred morning practices, such as taking time to be quiet and still before you start your day in prayer, meditation, and with a gratitude journal.*
- *Having regular and consistent sacred evening practices, such as a guided evening meditation, spending time outside gazing at the night sky, and making love.*
- *Speaking positive words and thinking positive thoughts.*
- *Focusing only on love and gratitude.*

ACKNOWLEDGING PAST LIVES

"Our souls existed before we were born and continue to exist after we die. And the process of being reborn continues over and over as our souls evolve spiritually."
~Dr. Brian Weiss on Oprah's Super Soul Sunday

We have had many past lives. We are going through an evolution of consciousness and are here to grow spiritually, to open more to love and see beyond the illusion of separateness, to open to the truth of wholeness and interconnectedness.

Past lives exist. Some believe this and others do not because it cannot be proven scientifically. Additionally, some believe it is helpful to know a past life or lives and others do not because we do not want to get stuck in a past life and wallow in it when what is important is our current life.

A good example of a past life is of a soul who is born and as a child has amazing talents, such as a child prodigy. This child can play the piano like a master or sing like an angel with no lessons and when they begin taking lessons, they surpass all their peers. This could be and is likely because of a past life, although many could argue they were just born with this as a gift from God. This is true too, however, I believe the skill they are so good at in this life came from experience in a past life. This is why practices and habits are so important. It is something to consider.

> **Invitation:** *Contemplate the following questions:*
> - *Are you open to the possibility that you have lived before?*
> - *Is your soul eternal and your body a vessel?*
> - *Could past lives be a part of your evolutionary process as a soul?*

Stacie Ivey

CHAPTER 12

LIVING A PURPOSE FILLED LIFE

"We must be willing to let go of the life we planned, so as to have the life that is waiting for us."
~Joseph Campbell

We are here to live out our purpose. Each of us has a unique set of purposes to fulfill. We are each imprinted with unique gifts that no one else has, and when we discover and begin to live from the place of our Divine life purpose, we discover our destiny. In a sense, we are already living it because even the paths of suffering are meant to jolt us back to the path of oneness. There is a natural order to the universe and we are intimately connected with it. There is nothing that happens by accident. Every experience has a purpose. Some experiences are to heal wounds and karmic debts, but ultimately all roads lead us back to our reconnection with the Divine and living out our life purpose.

"This is your gift, my dear. I want you to share it with the world. Be not afraid, for I am with you. I have been and always will be. I will never forsake you. Be still. Be still and know that I am God."
~Channeled message

Simply put, our Divine life purpose is to be here now in this moment, beyond the past and future projections of the mind and see that our lives are a gift. When we see that, we can recognize we are here to tap into and take action towards our unique way of living and serving the world. When we live from the awareness that we are one with all of life and the Divine, we live from a place of love, rather than a place of fear. The belief in separateness from the whole comes from fear. In knowing that we are interconnected and one with every leaf, every blade of grass, every insect, animal and human, then we can approach our lives from a place of love. From that place, ease, grace and flow become natural, because we are connected to the Divine within, which is our natural state.

"Tell me, what is it you plan to do with your one wild and precious life?"
~Mary Oliver

We are given the gift of life and it is our choice how to live it. Our lives are a direct reflection of our inner state. Whatever we believe is what we create. Whatever is unhealed within us rises up through some form of suffering as an invitation to be seen and heard so it can be transformed from something that holds us back to something that ignites us to reach our goals.

Invitation: *Contemplate the following questions:*
- *Where are you placing your attention throughout the day?*
- *What are your goals and aspirations?*
- *What is your soul calling you to?*
- *Are you doing things daily that get you on the path to that goal?*

CONNECTING TO DESIRE

"When you want something, all the universe conspires in helping you to achieve it."
~Paulo Coelho

What do you desire? Is your heart longing for a life filled with purpose, someone to love, a child, a healthy body, financial abundance or even clarity on something? Whatever it is, first ask,

Why do I want this?

Then, if your desire is coming from a place of pure heart, feel it as if it is already here.

STEP 1

Speak it, write it, connect it to a positive emotion, and feel it in your body now as if it's here now. Say affirmations in the present tense. When you say something like, "I want to find my soul mate," you are placing the belief in something outside of you to fulfill you and it will always be "out there." Instead, say "I have a passionate, harmonious and loving relationship with my ideal partner now."

STEP 2

Take action from the place of belief. This is where you are given guidance when you learn to quiet the mind and listen at deeper and deeper levels. You prepare, and then suddenly synchronicities, which appear in the form of people, places and things, step up to meet you and help you along the way. It is the place where miracles and magic appear to happen, and often they happen in the most surprising and unexpected ways. For example, you may be at a park and just happen to meet someone who is the person or knows of the person you need to meet next that will help you take the next step toward your dream.

STEP 3

Surrender. In the bible (NIV), Matthew, 7:7, states, "Ask and it will be given to you; seek, and you will find; knock and the door will be opened to you." These are profound words. What these words tell us is all we need to do is speak the words for what our hearts long for, seek through God, and take action. Then we must step back and trust the Divine to take over. This is where surrender comes in. The God who can be named is not God, so the words used to refer to God in this book are only signposts to the Source of all life, which connects us all. It is who and what we are returning to. It is why we are here.

Life is a miracle and we all have a unique and profound reason for being here. When we put our focused attention on what we want, take the steps necessary to achieve it, and then surrender, it is possible. With God, everything is possible.

Invitation:

- *Set an intention.*
- *Connect it to your feelings.*
- *Focus your energy on it for 60 seconds.*
- *Journal and track your progress daily.*
- *Continue this practice for 21 days.*
- *Check your progress and make any shifts or adjustments you deem necessary.*
- *Pray and ask for guidance if needed.*

SEEK OUT WHAT INSPIRES YOU

*"When you're following your energy and doing what you want all the
time, the distinction between work and play dissolves."*
~Shakti Gawain

The soul knows what it likes and needs and carries a wisdom
beyond the level of understanding that only the mind can
provide. It is beyond the mind. When you are listening, you
are feeling in alignment with what you are doing, who you are
with and where you are going. When you're not, you know it,
but you may not know it at first. It could take some time of
shedding the layers of conditioning and false ideas about who
you are to get there, but parts of you know you are already
connected to your purpose, always. You never have to doubt
that the journey that you are on is exactly where you need to
be at all times.

Invitation:

- *Find art that you love and put it on your walls.*
- *Create a vision board of what inspires you, without
  thinking too much about it.*
- *Listen to your body when you feel you need to rest or
  eat better.*
- *Be courageous and brave to pursue the dreams you
  have, or at least open to learning what they are if you
  don't already know.*

LEANING INTO FEAR

*"And the day came when the risk to remain tight in a bud was more
painful than the risk it took to blossom."*
~Anais Nin

We crave certainty. It makes us feel safe. We want to know how to know when something's going to happen, how it's going to happen, where it's going to happen and why.

Certainty is familiarity. It tells us what to expect. We like when we know what's coming next. But life doesn't always work that way, does it? For a while, we can go on with the status quo, but then something happens, usually a loss of some sort that jolts us into a new reality. At first, this new reality feels empty. It takes us to a place that's unfamiliar and possibly scary or into a realm where we don't know who we are anymore.

Trusting the flow of the universe feels like jumping off a cliff. The primal part of our brain tells us, "NO! Don't go there! It isn't safe!" But what if it was? What if no matter what happened next, it was going to be ok?

We operate out of our old ways of thinking, our old conditioning, including our global, local, sexual, religious, family, and generational conditioning. It's not bad or good, it just is. When we bring awareness to this, it is the first step to moving beyond it.

For the longest time, I resisted following my life's purpose. I resisted hearing my inner guidance and when I finally got quiet enough to hear, I resisted the messages I received. Resistance was my best friend and worst enemy rolled into one. I had a strong inner saboteur telling me I didn't have enough time, money, clarity, focus, organization, or wisdom to do what I wanted to do. It wasn't until I learned to listen to and follow the wisdom of my inner voice instead of my saboteur or "mean girl" that things started to change. I let my "mean girl" be seen, but not have decision making abilities. My inner "mean girl" is simply the scared and conditioned part of me who was just trying to protect me and keep me safe. I decided to allow her to have her place at the table, where she could be seen and acknowledged, but she wasn't allowed to have decision making abilities any longer.

We are all meant to live the life of our dreams. We are all meant to be happy. We are all connected to a source and life force energy that flows through us at all times. What is needed is to bring our attention and awareness to this energy. When we do, we begin to trust. When we take steps in the right direction, we begin to trust more. If we step off our path, the universe has a way of self-correcting.

> **Invitation:** *Allow yourself to connect with your breath. When you focus your awareness on your breath, you can control your breath, but when you aren't focused on your breath, what happens? Are you still breathing? What is the force that is making that happen? What is the energy that runs through you and makes up all that you are? Open to the possibilities of what you don't know you don't know. This is where the mystery lies. This is where God/Goddess is.*

STEPPING OUT OF BEING STUCK

"Fear is the glue that keeps you stuck. Faith is the solvent that sets you free."
~Shannon L. Alder

Nothing has ever been fully stagnant. It is always moving or changing, in one way or another. When something becomes stagnant, we feel it and know something needs to change. The question is not whether the change will occur, but rather when. It is time for something new to manifest in physical form.

When we feel stuck, especially around pursuing our life purpose, we should ask, "What is holding me back?" Often, the answer is fear associated with survival. Deeply ingrained in all of us is a fear that we won't be provided for, that our ideas won't work, and so on. Ultimately, we are not trusting life when we are in this place. Rather, when we shift to taking baby steps on a regular and consistent basis, everything begins to open up to what we need at the exact perfect time, including resources, people, and anything else we need.

Invitation: *You are naturally creative and a co-creator with the Divine. Begin to express yourself in ways that fuel you and branch those out into being of service to share them with others. Your soul knows why you are here. The first step is to begin somewhere. You will be led. All you need to do is trust. Ideas to start:*

- *Begin writing your book.*
- *Start doing whatever you are called to do for a small exchange at first, even if it's for free. You are learning and that is invaluable.*
- *Do anything creative that fuels you, such as painting, creating jewelry, working with essential oils, dressing in a way that feels good, and so on.*
- *Rest, play and enjoy. Make your life a service filled with joy. When you are tapped into and living your life purpose, you look forward to work because your work is one with your play.*
- *Remember, you are Divine, the I AM, and the daughter of Father God and Mother Goddess in one. You are the Goddess and here for a beautiful and unique reason that only you can share in your unique way. Life is your gift and you are a gift in this precious life to this world.*

WILLINGNESS

"We don't always succeed in what we try, certainly not by the world's standards, but I think you'll find it's the willingness to keep trying that matters most."
~Fred Rogers (Mister Rogers)

Willingness is the opening to what you don't know you don't know. When we are willing, we trust trying a new and different approach in hopes of seeing a different result.

The dictionary defines willingness as the quality or state of being prepared to do something. It is being ready and having the courage to take action when you fear the action won't result in success. Whatever your fear, willingness is the action of facing your fears and instead of running from them, it is a leaning into them. When we lean into what we are afraid of, fear loses its power over us.

Our internal survival mechanism is designed to protect us from what is dangerous. The false belief our mind tells us is that something is dangerous, when it actually is not. It feels dangerous because it is scary to put yourself out there. It is a place of vulnerability. It is a place of authenticity.

Anyone who has achieved greatness has had to lean into their fear many times and had the tenacity and desire to keep pushing forward, even amongst hundreds or thousands of rejections. Those who are willing to believe in their dreams and take action steps toward them without giving up, accomplish them.

Invitation: Ask yourself, where am I holding myself back from my own power? What thoughts or beliefs do I hold onto that don't serve me? What belief is keeping me from a willingness to keep trying?

TAKING ACTION

"The path to success is to take massive, determined actions."
~Tony Robbins

In order to accomplish anything, we want to feel, see, hear, taste, smell and touch in the physical world, it is essential to take action on the inspiration or idea that is given to us at the time it is given. It can feel like an overwhelming or difficult task to bring into full manifested form something that starts as just a concept or idea, but it doesn't have to be. All we have to do is take the first step, then the next step and so on. It's like driving a car at night and only being able to see as far ahead as the headlights show the road ahead. That's all we need because that's all that is being shown. Yet it's important to not do anything, thinking it's too hard or it won't happen or whatever other excuse we may want to come up with to sabotage the idea. We must trust and have patience. Just like planting any seed, it may take a little time, but not always. Sometimes things are instantly manifested and other times they aren't.

For example, have you ever thought of someone or something and then all of the sudden they called you or it showed up as if by magic?

Invitations:
- *Prioritize your goals.*
- *Stay focused.*
- *Know that each and every action toward the desired goal is important, no matter how big or small.*
- *Have consistency and follow through.*
- *Believe it's possible.*
- *Be patient.*
- *Know your contribution and dreams matter and you are here to bring them forward to share with others.*

- *Believe in acceleration. We are opening to more and more possibilities and there has never been a better time to bring forward every dream necessary for the world to thrive forward.*
- *Trust Divine timing.*

DIVINE TIMING

"Prayer is powerful. But remember that God works in His timing, not yours."
~Sera Beak

There is our human desire for timing and then there is Divine timing. Divine timing is beyond time and where the present moment sits. Each moment is only the present moment.

When we want something, it is important for us to begin by planting the seeds towards our dreams and desires, and then we must wait. We must be patient and allow, knowing there are forces working behind and through the scenes that we are not aware of. This is where trust comes in.

Divine timing is above and within all. It is the eagle's eye view that we may not see now. When we are going through something, often we want to see change or results immediately, but often they aren't immediate. This is because it is not time yet. Our job is to do what we can do and not give up just because we don't see immediate results. The desire for immediate results comes from our "fast food" culture, which also gives us a sense of entitlement. When we trust Divine timing, sometimes it may be immediate.

Invitation: Surrender it to the Divine and do your part. You will likely be in awe of the results the more you practice this spiritual habit.

THE EMBODIMENT OF YOUR GREATNESS

"If you ask me what I came to do in this world. I, as an artist, will answer you: I am here to live out loud."
~Emile Zola

As women, we were born with natural talents and gifts. What we naturally do as children is who we are. It is important to remember and connect to that inner child that was fearless and knew who we were before the conditioning began. This includes the messages we received from our parents that were uncomfortable to them, so they repressed it in ourselves through actions and words.

I always felt like a leader, but it was repressed in me through my mother calling me "bossy."

When we shine the light on what we need to release, we can become free to truly be who we are meant to be. What needs to be released can be held anywhere in the body, but our power center is held in our solar plexus or core. Additionally, as women, healing and renewing our connection to our womb space is critical. Many women have fears around this and stuck energy due to past abuses that may or may not even belong to them. Guided meditation, pranayama (breath-work) and yoga can help heal these wounds.

Invitation: *To embody your greatness, the key is knowing you are Divine and not the small identity you thought you were. Here are some tools to help:*
- *Stand upright and confidently walk through the day knowing you are unique and have a right to be here.*
- *Pay attention to your body language. Do you fold inward to stay small or do you project your power and light like a magnet of unique brilliance?*

- *Remember that you teach through your presence and actions, first and foremost.*
- *Trust in the power of your words. Say and think positive affirmations, pray and speak only positive.*
- *Write down your daily, weekly, monthly and yearly goals. Place them in your calendar or planner. This takes your ideas and brings them into the physical world. It is a necessary beginning step.*
- *Each night, review and write down any new goals for tomorrow.*
- *Meditate daily, ideally first thing in the morning and right before sleep in the evening.*
- *Try this meditation. Place your hands on your womb space and breath in and out for a few breaths. Then move your hands to your heart and take a few more breaths. Finally, place your index and middle fingers at the point between your eyebrows and breathe again for 2-3 deep breaths.*
- *Be here in each breath and present moment as much as you can remember to. When you find yourself projecting into the past and future, come back to your breath with a simple inhale and exhale. Breathe deeply.*
- *Slow down and listen to silence.*
- *Follow through with what you started.*
- *Cherish and honor your friendships.*
- *Build community. There is truly strength in numbers and each of us has something to share.*
- *Feel beautiful and love your life.*
- *Love yourself unconditionally, which means embracing all of you…everything!*

SERVICE: MAKING YOUR LIFE A PRAYER OF SERVICE

"Don't you know yet? It is your light that lights the world."
~Rumi

Live in service. Give selflessly, without expecting anything in return. When you give in this way, you actually get back more than you could have ever expected to get. There in lies the dichotomy. When you give selflessly, you receive back in ways beyond your wildest dreams. Giving free from expectation is true giving. This doesn't mean to never ask for money for your services, because this can be a problem too. What it means is to let your wisdom guide you. Let your spirit lead the way. Let the Divine come in, so that you may be a channel for peace. Let grace come in, so that you may be a channel for love.

"Try to be a rainbow in someone's cloud."
~Maya Angelou

Our lives are not our own. We are here to be of service. We are here to be happy. We are here to love one another. We are here to see beyond the colors of our skins, the separations of our egos, and separateness in general. We are here to be one with all of life and to recognize we are one with all. We are here to be happy and enjoy life. The belief that we are separate from this connection to all is the cause of our unhappiness. Our belief in separateness is an illusion. It is a lie. This idea comes from the ego. Ego serves a purpose, but doesn't serve us when it gets out of balance.

We are meant to step out of our comfort zones. We are meant to shine. We are meant to step out of the small boxes we put ourselves in.

Invitations:

- *What would you give if you could give anything?*
- *What would you do for work if money was no object?*
- *Practice random acts of kindness, such as extending a smile or a hand to someone in need.*
- *Volunteer.*
- *Give money to a cause you believe in.*
- *Tell someone you care about them.*
- *Give without expecting anything in return.*

MANIFESTING DREAMS

"Dreams are illustrations from the book your soul is writing about you."
~Marsha Norman

We would not have the individual and collective dreams we have if it weren't possible, or even more, *necessary* for us to reach those dreams. The dream you have is yours and meant to be manifested and brought into the world.

Dreams are not only real; they are highly important in the world. We are each meant to shine and share our unique gifts. They are uniquely ours and no one can fulfill the unique gift that each of us individually is meant to share. Then, as individuals, we are able to step into the collective sharing, giving and receiving that transforms the world!

Our dreams, both individually and collectively, are more than possible, they are required in order for us to fulfill our Divine destiny and to step more fully into our life purpose to be fully who we are.

> **Invitation:** *Ask yourself, what is my soul calling me forth to do? Do you hear the calling within you? Are you trying to put yourself into a box or are you willing to listen and then take the action steps necessary for positive change in your life and in the world? You cannot do this alone and you will be supported every step of the way. Take the first step.*

CO-CREATING A NEW EARTH

What you really know is possible in your hearts is possible. We make it
possible by our will. What we imagine in our minds becomes our world.
That's just one of the many things I've learned about water.
~Masuru Emoto

We are entering a new time on Earth where it is critical to choose love over fear, collaboration over competition, and innovation over the status quo. As we evolve, we must connect to our imaginations in order to create a world that works for all. Never before have humans faced the challenges we are facing today at the scale and depth we are facing them. We face crisis on the levels of government, economy, health care, and the Earth. Now critical resources that we once took for granted, such as water, threaten our very survival and it's happening on such a scale that we may feel disempowered with what to do about it. We are literally on the Titanic with the iceberg right in front of us, and if we choose fear, we are frozen because of it, but if we choose love, we can create anything we need. This is why it is so important to stay focused on love to shut the door on fear.

Invitation:

- *Don't allow yourself to get overwhelmed by the problems in the world.*
- *Think globally but act locally. Start in your local community and then branch out.*
- *Take small steps toward where you are being called to serve. This can range from starting your own garden, to creating women's circles, to teaching a class in something you enjoy.*
- *Build your community of support and find others interested in helping you reach your goals.*
- *Trust that if you keep moving forward, you will meet your mark.*

You are ready.

You are beautiful.

You are whole and complete.

You are perfect just as you are.

Go after your dreams.

Now is the time.

With so much love,

Stacie

Stacie Ivey

BIBLIOGRAPHY

Aon Prakasha, Padma and Aon Prakasha, Anaiya, *Womb Wisdom: Awakening the creative and forgotten powers of the feminine* (Destiny Books, 2011)

Aron, Elaine, *The Highly Sensitive Person: How to thrive when the world overwhelms you* (Broadway Books, 1997)

Aron, Elaine, *The Highly Sensitive Child: Helping children thrive when the world overwhelms them* (Broadway Books, 2002)

Beak, Sera, *The Red Book: A deliciously unorthodox approach to igniting your divine spark* (Jossey Bass, 2006)

Cameron, Julia, *The Artist's Way: A spiritual path to higher creativity* (Jeremy P. Tarcher/Perigee, 1992)

Campbell, Joseph, *The Hero with a Thousand Faces* (Princeton University Press, 1972)

Hay, Louise, *You Can Heal Your Life* (Hay House, 1987)

Kubler-Ross, Elisabeth, *On Death and Dying* (The Macmillan Company, 1969)

Myss, Caroline M., *Sacred Contracts: Awakening your divine potential* (Harmony Books, 2001)

Sri Swami Satchidananda, *The Yoga Sutras of Patanjali* (Integral Yoga Publications; Reprint edition, September, 2012)

Stacie Ivey

ACKNOWLEDGEMENTS

This book has been an evolutionary process for me. It has gone through numerous titles and restructuring. It has grown and deepened as I have grown and deepened. There were many times I thought it would never be finished because I was stuck in fear. I had all of the typical thoughts of my inner mean girl, such as, "Who am I to write this book? Who do I think I am? I don't possibly know enough. I'm not an enlightened master. What if no one reads it? What if no one likes it? What if it upsets people? What if people question me on things I can't answer?" My inner saboteur would also come in and create drama in my life, which would block my creativity. So, in the process of writing this book, I had to learn patience, perseverance, structure, focus, and willingness. I had to learn everything I wrote about, and I am still learning and growing, as we all are.

To my beautiful daughter, Karenna, you are stunning inside and out. Your intelligence is second to none and you can do anything you want with the gifts you have been given. Never forget the beautiful light inside you and don't be afraid to let it shine. Approach your life with wonder and amazement. Everything you need to succeed is already within you. Know the messages of this world are not always true and some are meant to keep you small. Be discerning. Take risks. Love fully. Trust your instinct. I love you more than you can imagine.

To my amazing son, Aidan, I love your creativity, intelligence, drive, and authenticity. You are such a bright light who truly cares and loves deeply while reminding us all to have fun in the process. Your talents and gifts give you the ability to share yourself with the world and make an impact in a huge way. I love how you make friends effortlessly and have a way of connecting with people more than anyone else I know. Keep your heart open and know your sensitivity is a strength. You are a blessing and gift to me beyond what I could ever express in words. You have my heart.

To my beloved husband James, thank you for choosing me to share in this life adventure with you. I am grateful for your patience and support in giving me the space and time I needed to write this book. You are a bright light and gift to all who enter your world. I love your sense of fun, romance, curiosity, exploration and adventure. You remind me to stay playful and not take myself so seriously. I love you with all my heart.

To all my mothers, grandmothers and aunts, I am so blessed to have learned all the lessons I have learned from you. Thank you for teaching me grace, nurturing, compassion, generosity, creativity, joy, a love of nature, and presence. I love your cooking and the way you have made me feel safe, secure and loved without conditions.

Donna, mom, thank you for choosing me to be your daughter. Even though I became your daughter through adoption, you are my mother through and through. I cherish our family and am lucky beyond compare to have grown up with such support and love. Thank you for your openness, generosity and wisdom. You have always been there for me, listened to my joys and cries, and supported me through it all. I love you!

Eileen, my biological mother, I love you. When I met you and my extended family for the first time, the missing puzzle pieces of my life were filled. Thank you for selflessly choosing the best life for me and for being in my life now. You welcomed me back as if I had never left and have shown me a new meaning of unconditional love. I feel so blessed and lucky for my adoption journey. Never regret anything. Everything happens just as it should.

Donna, Eileen, Isabel, and Anne, thank you for being Karenna and Aidan's grandmothers. I am so grateful for you and for your unconditional love and wisdom.

Grandma Anne, thank you for teaching me about life, generosity, and that angels are real. You are the best Italian cook ever and I look forward to seeing your 100th birthday! I love you so much.

Aunt Judy, thank you for always listening to and supporting me and of course, letting me be your "favorite niece!"

To all my fathers, grandfathers and uncles, thank you loving me fully and holding the space for me to be me.

Larry, dad, thank you for teaching me how to ride a bike and drive a car. Thank you for telling me I can do anything I want in this life. I love that we went camping on a regular basis in our Coachman motor home on our trips around Arizona and to the beach in Mexico. You and mom made childhood for Toby and I so much fun. Thank you for selflessly providing for your family without wanting or needing anything for yourself. You have taught me what is possible for a father to be and the example for all men. To you, I am so grateful.

Grandpa James, thank you for teaching me about the Great Depression through your personal stories about turtle soup lines, for showing me you can use as much syrup as you want on pancakes and for loving my grandma so completely.

Martin, thank you for being the father of our children.

John, thank you for welcoming me with such open arms and for telling me I will always be your daughter.

To my brothers, sisters, girlfriends, boyfriends, and all of the women, men, and children I have met along the way in this life, thank you for being you. I feel beyond blessed for the beautiful spontaneous meetings which have sometimes turned into lasting friendships and long-term relationships. Thank you for loving and accepting me as me. I thank each of you for the profound impact you have made in my life.

Toby, thank you for being adopted with me and growing up as my brother. We had a lot of fun adventures and I love you. You are an amazing father to Alynn and Orion and husband to Lisa.

Jennifer, Jonathan and Brian, thank you for loving and accepting me as your biological sister when we found each other again in adulthood. Your unconditional love and acceptance of me will never be forgotten. I love you!

Lisa, Nikki and Tracy, thank you for being my sisters through marriage and for all of your love and support. Theresa, thank you for bringing your son into this world and for being my mother in law. Alysa, thank you for accepting me the way you have and for your dad. I love you all so much.

To my nieces and nephews, especially Orion, Alynn, Ember, Katlyn, Jacob, Samantha, and Daniel, I love seeing the world through your eyes and am truly blessed to be your aunt.

Amy Collette, my editor, thank you for your unending guidance and patience with me as I went through this process. You supported me with such boundless compassion, curiosity, and joy. Thank you for your book, *The Gratitude Connection*, and for leading the way for me and other authors (amycollette.com).

Nancy Rynes, thank you for your creativity and beautiful interior book design (nancyrynes.com).

Ted Roach, thank you for your wonderful help and professionalism with my interior book design updates.

To Mother and Father God, thank you for showing me my true Self. Thank you for all of my lessons and struggles, for I see how they came through me to bring me closer to You. I understand how I needed to process and heal my own shadows and darkness in order to be a conduit for Your light to enter. Your love is limitless and I am humbled by the moments I have let myself open to and slow down enough to feel Your expansive and omnipresent love. You have shown yourself to me in some of the most unexpected moments and in the most profound and beautiful ways. Your love is eternal and everlasting, beyond all human suffering. I am in awe of You.

Stacie Ivey

ABOUT THE AUTHOR

Stacie Ivey, M.S., is a nationally certified and licensed speech-language pathologist, registered yoga instructor, and speaker. Through many personal life struggles and her own inner promptings, Stacie began exploring yoga, spirituality, personal development, mindfulness, energy healing and embodiment practices to heal and transform her own life. She now mentors women, sensitives, empaths and spiritual seekers to heal and discover their inner truth by connecting to sacred wisdom and the Divine Feminine. Stacie works with individuals and groups through private sessions, retreats, and workshops. She lives with her family in Albuquerque, NM. **www.stacieivey.com**

Stacie Ivey

Made in the USA
San Bernardino, CA
15 July 2018